FRENCH GIRL *knits*

KRISTEEN GRIFFIN-GRIMES

Editor, Ann Budd
Cover and interior design, Karla Baker
Photography, Joe Hancock
Technical editor, Lori Gayle
Illustrations, Gayle Ford
Production design, Katherine Jackson

Interweave Press LLC
201 East Fourth Street
Loveland, CO 80537-5655 USA
interweavebooks.com

Printed in China by Asia Pacific Offset.

Library of Congress Cataloging-in-Publication Data

Griffin-Grimes, Kristeen, 1947-
  French girl knits : innovative techniques, romantic details,
and feminine designs / Kristeen Griffin-Grimes, author.
      p. cm.
  Includes index.
  ISBN 978-1-59668-069-2 (pbk.)
  1. Knitting--Patterns. 2. France--In art. I. Title.
  TT825.G6835 2009
  746.43'2041--dc22

                              2008020564

10 9 8 7 6 5 4 3 2 1

acknowledgments

So many thanks go out to these lovely people who supported me through the writing of this book.
I was welcomed like family by the entire Interweave team: Steve, Marilyn, Rebecca, Anne, Annie, Laura, Tiffany, Eunny, and Linda. Deepest gratitude to my editors, Tricia Waddell and Ann Budd—your stellar vision, guidance, and friendship made me doubly thankful to be working with you.

My dear family, Phil, Rain, and Deva kept me afloat in so many ways with their love and wise counsel and are now happy that I can return to being *chef de cuisine* instead of *chef de tricot*.

Special thanks to the yarn companies, large and small, that generously provided me with the most beautiful fibers with which to dream and create; I am delighted by our continuing partnership. The French Girl team of knitters who gave their time to work on some designs in this book deserve extra *bisous:* Monica Welle-Brown (Paloma and Sophia), Emily Munson (Celeste), and Karen Mortensen (Cybèle), as well as the test knitters for my design collections: Amy Tyer, Mary Ann Peach, Sheryl Means, Ellen Gowey, and Anne Allgood . . . *merci, mes amis!*

When I returned to knitting after a long break, my Rowan sales rep, Sandy Blue, encouraged me to market my designs . . . her early support set me on a path that lead to writing this book, and for that I am eternally thankful!

I also salute the behind-the-scenes magicians who clipped, curled, and whipped this book into shape: Joe Hancock (photographer), Pamela Norman (art direction), Carol Beaver (stylist), and Catherine Corona (hair and makeup).

Technical editor Lori Gayle deserves my highest and most humble praise—there would be no book without her. The garments I designed were very challenging to translate into multiple sizes due to their unique one-piece construction; she rose to the occasion and smoothed all the wrinkles from my sometimes imperfect efforts—bless you Lori!

Thanks also to the many knitters and crocheters who have supported my design company, French Girl, over the last years by purchasing patterns and making up their own dazzling versions.

The shops that carry French Girl patterns also have my deepest thanks. Special hugs to my dear friend Susan Cropper from Loop in London for our shared love of all things gorgeous and girly.

My talented chiropractor kept me (literally) on the straight and narrow—thank you, Dr. David Kirdahy!

For allowing me to share their lovely Paris engagement story for Bijou, merci, Andrea and David!

En fin, a petite valentine to our family's adopted home, La Belle France, whose original draw was born in the blood and now lives on through our tours and French Girl. I am forever thankful I was given the opportunity to travel to your shores, dine on the bounty of your land, and have my eyes opened by the enduring beauty of your country—*Vive la France!*

TABLE OF *contents*

BONJOUR *from french girl*

My passion for clothing design began in the 1960s with a skirt—humble and faded black with oversized buttons—plucked from the racks of the local Goodwill store. Why my mother chose it for me is still a mystery, considering her love for the glamorous 1940s gowns she wore as a swing-era jazz vocalist. In my cavernous urban school, faced with a gang of sixth-grade girls smartly outfitted in the latest knife-pleated kilts and matching sweaters, my sad little black skirt didn't stand a chance. As I glanced at the tattered buttonholes held together with safety pins, I had a quintessential "Scarlett O'Hara moment," I promised myself, paraphrasing Scarlett's words from *Gone With the Wind*—"I'll never wear ugly clothes again!"

Along with my sisters, I learned to sew and, through trial (needles plunged into fingers), error (sleeves sewn on inside out and backward), and tribulation, we triumphed. By the time I was fifteen, most of my clothes were "Vogue Originals" translated into the fabrics of the day, as well as some garments fashioned from my own imaginings. Learning to knit, crochet, and spin soon followed during my back-to-the-land days in the 1970s.

New World French culture settled deep in my bones as I was growing up—a lively mélange of aromatic Cajun gumbo and New Orleans jazz tunes that found its way into every corner of our family's sprawling Seattle home. The mystique of my mother's exotic childhood saturated my early life as well. Her recollections of singing in the smoke-tinged French quarter jazz clubs of the 1930s all seemed terribly romantic. When I was very young I longed to visit the French "motherland." I spent hours tracing its roughly hexagonal borders in the well-worn atlas or trying to speak a faux

French gleaned from the few phrases my parents tossed back and forth.

Many years later, my own family of four crossed the border into France for the first time and something that had long been dormant switched on. I had at last found a place that made sense, one that elevated the ordinary into art: the perfectly mounded, Rubenesque aubergines glistening in the sun at midday market; the precisely decorated shop windows displaying petite children's shoes, classic shaving brushes, and frilly seed packets. I began to understand more fully what could be done with very little. The French were masters of an art that had nothing to do with money and everything to do with an appreciation of the small, lovely moments in life.

After days spent trying to capture that illusive French aesthetic on film and notepad, my mind buzzing with sensual overload, I returned home deeply inspired to infuse my life with all things beautiful. This soon translated into a rejuvenated interest in the needle arts and the luscious fibers that had begun to appear in the marketplace. New-to-me yarns from esteemed British merchant Rowan beckoned; vibrant hand-dyeds from South America's Manos del Uruguay sealed the deal. After hours of dreaming and planning, I launched my design company, French Girl, in 2005. It has now expanded to include the tours our family leads in the French countryside, sharing our passion for *La Belle France* with others who love rustic cuisine, wine, and, of course, knitting!

Most of my designs involve seamless construction, such as taught by Barbara Walker and Elizabeth Zimmermann. Although I adore sewing, the idea of a completely seamless garment is infinitely appealing, the added benefit being the ability to custom fit along the way. If you're accustomed to knitting garments in pieces and rigorously following a printed pattern word for word, seamless construction will open up a new world of knitting possibilities. Not only is the knitting easier—no wrong-side rows to deal with; no seams to sew—it's a snap to make adjustments along the way for a custom fit. The five construction overviews scattered throughout this book cover my favorite methods for one-piece knitting.

Although this book focuses on my designs, I encourage to "learn by doing" and make your own design decisions. To that end, please avail yourself of the many articles, books, and websites listed in the Bibliography on page 157. As you work up the projects in *French Girl Knits*, I hope you're inspired to hone your seamless skills, taking time to custom fit your garments and create something enduringly beautiful.

—Bon tricot, mes amis!

la boutique PARISIENNE

ROMANTIC AND VINTAGE INSPIRED

You happen upon a tiny jewel of a shop tucked away down a quiet tree-shaded lane. Strange, you never noticed it before. Yet there in the twinkling window is "The Dress," the one that whispers to you (in French, of course), the one that you must have, the one that will have you eating on the cheap for a month, the one that says, "You!" Oh, to find such a dress today.

I can only imagine what Paris must have been like after the privations of the Second World War gave way to a burst of fresh, hopeful energy. Dior and the New Look. Chanel and Givenchy. The Capitol abuzz with opulent fabrics and trims, buttons, sashes, and other adornments. Silk stockings again. And mountains of chocolate, sugar, and butter!

If you happen to own a vintage piece, take note of the detailing and the precise stitches found in both sewn and knitted garments. In La Boutique Parisienne, I hope to capture the feminine silhouette and color palette of a bygone era with designs that will let you fashion graceful, figure-enhancing garments. Picture yourself on a tranquil afternoon with no to-do list, indulging in the joy of sensuous yarn and hours of peaceful knitting. Take some time to create something beautiful for yourself. *Bienvenue à La Boutique Parisienne!*

SATINE ✳ *floaty tunic tank*

The brocante, or secondhand markets, of France are legendary for the most unexpected finds. They can provide mini-history lessons as you walk their aisles. The textiles call out to me: starched, white, beautifully preserved, and expertly stitched, they are poignant reminders of all things past.

Satine takes its shape from a vintage chemise found on market day in a tiny village in the South of France. The lure of the nostalgic is powerful—and not just for me. I've seen some very modern French girls gathering up armloads of these beauties to cart home. The seamstress who fashioned the muse for Satine took time to embellish the neckline and armholes with delicate floral embroidery, even though the garment was worn under layers of clothing.

This feathery mohair/silk tunic is constructed in one piece, worked from the bottom up, with waist and bust shaped by using progressively smaller and then larger needles. You can alter the length to make the tunic more dresslike by adding rounds before the waist shaping.

FINISHED SIZE

30¼ (35¾, 41¼)" (77 [91, 104.5] cm) bust circumference. Sweater shown measures 30¼" (77 cm). NOTE: This garment is designed with 2" to 3" (5 to 7.5 cm) negative wearing ease for a close, body-conscious fit in the bust area.

YARN

Worsted weight (#4 Medium) and sport-weight (#2 Fine).

SHOWN HERE: Rowan Kidsilk Aura (75% kid mohair, 25% silk; 82 yd [75 ml/25 g]: #757 vintage (MC; lilac), 4 (5, 6) skeins. Rowan Kidsilk Night (67% kid mohair, 18% silk, 10% polyester, 5% nylon; 227 yd [208 ml/25 g]: #607 starlight (CC; white), 1 skein for all sizes. NOTE: This yarn has been discontinued; substitute the laceweight mohair/silk yarn of your choice.

NEEDLES

LOWER BODY: size U.S. 13 (9 mm): 36" (90 cm) circular (cir). EMPIRE-WAIST SHAPING AND UPPER BODY: size U.S. 11 (8 mm): 24" and 36" (60 and 90 cm) cir. NECK FINISHING: size U.S. 10½ (6.5 mm): 24" (60 cm) cir. *Adjust needle size if necessary to obtain the correct gauge.*

NOTIONS

Markers (m); stitch holders; tapestry needle; size J/10 (6 mm) crochet hook.

GAUGE

24 stitches and 16 rounds (2 pattern repeats wide and 8 pattern repeats high) = 8½" (21.5 cm) wide and 5½" (14 cm) high in 12-stitch lace pattern with MC on largest needle, after blocking; 24 stitches and 16 rounds (3 pattern repeats wide and 8 pattern repeats high) = 8¼" (21 cm) wide and 5" (12.5 cm) high in 8-stitch lace pattern with MC on middle-size needles, after blocking.

Notes

- The lower body is worked in the round to the armholes. Stitches at the base of the armholes are put on holders, and additional stitches are cast on over the armhole gaps for the shoulder straps. The upper body and straps are worked in the round to the neck edge.
- During blocking, the straps are curved up at each side to frame the scooped neckline.

Stitch Guide

SK2P

Sl 1 knitwise with yarn in back (kwise wyb), k2tog, pass slipped st over—2 sts dec'd.

12-STITCH LACE PATTERN *(MULTIPLE OF 12 STS)*

RND 1: *K1, yo, k4, sk2p, k4, yo; rep from * to end.

RND 2: Knit.

Repeat Rnds 1 and 2 for pattern, being careful not to drop the yarnover at end of Rnd 1.

8-STITCH LACE PATTERN *(MULTIPLE OF 8 STS)*

RND 1: *K1, yo, k2, sk2p, k2, yo; rep from * to end.

RND 2: Knit.

Repeat Rnds 1 and 2 for pattern, being careful not to drop the yarnover at end of Rnd 1.

Lower Body

With MC, largest cir needle, and using the cable method (see Glossary), CO 133 (157, 181) sts.

JOINING RND: Work Rnd 1 of 12-st lace patt (see Stitch Guide) to last st, place marker (pm) after final yo of last rep, and then join for working in rnds by knitting the last CO st tog with the first st (counts as first st of Rnd 2), being careful not to twist sts—132 (156, 180) sts. Knit to end of rnd to complete Rnd 2 of patt.

Work 26 (26, 28) rnds even, ending with Rnd 2 of patt—28 (28, 30) patt rnds completed; piece measures about 9¾ (9¾, 10¼)" (25 [25, 26] cm) from CO, or 2½" (6.5 cm) less than desired length to underbust. NOTE: To customize lower body length, work more or fewer repeats of lace pattern here; every 2 rounds added or removed will increase or decrease the length by about ¾" (2 cm). Change to longer middle-size cir needle and work 4 rnds even in patt.

FIRST DEC RND: *K1, yo, k1, ssk, k1, sk2p, k1, k2tog, k1, yo; rep from * to end—110 (130, 150) sts rem; each 12-st patt rep has been dec'd to 10 sts.

Knit 1 rnd.

SECOND DEC RND: *K1, yo, k1, ssk, sk2p, k2tog, k1, yo; rep from * to end, changing to shorter middle-size cir needle if necessary for your size—88 (104, 120) sts rem; each 10-st patt rep has been dec'd to 8 sts.

Knit 1 rnd and mark it as the underbust—piece measures about 12¼ (12¼, 12¾)″ (31 [31, 32.5] cm) from CO. Change to 8-st lace patt (see Stitch Guide) and work 16 (18, 20) rnds even, ending with Rnd 2 of patt—piece measures about 17¼ (18, 19)″ (44 [45.5, 48.5] cm) from CO, or 5 (5¾, 6¼)″ (12.5 [14.5, 16] cm) above underbust. NOTE: To customize the bust area, work more or fewer repeats of lace pattern here until piece fits as desired from underbust to underarms; every 2 rounds added or removed will increase or decrease bust area length by about ½″ (1.3 cm).

Upper Body and Shoulder Straps

Work 24 (32, 32) sts in patt for back, place next 16 (16, 24) sts on holder for left underarm, pm, use the cable method to CO 37 sts for left shoulder strap, with RS facing slip last CO st to left needle, pm, work slipped CO st tog with first st of front as k2tog (counts as first k1 of first patt rep), work 31 (39, 39) more sts in patt for front, place next 16 (16, 24) sts on holder for right underarm, pm, use the cable method to CO 37 sts for right shoulder strap, temporarily remove end-of-rnd m, with RS facing slip last CO st to left needle, replace end-of-rnd m, k2tog (last CO st tog with first st of rnd; counts as first st of Rnd 2)—128 (144, 144) sts; 24 (32, 32) back sts; 32 (40, 40) front sts; 36 sts each strap. Knit to end of rnd to complete Rnd 2, changing to longer middle-size cir needle if there are too many sts for your size to fit comfortably on the shorter cir.

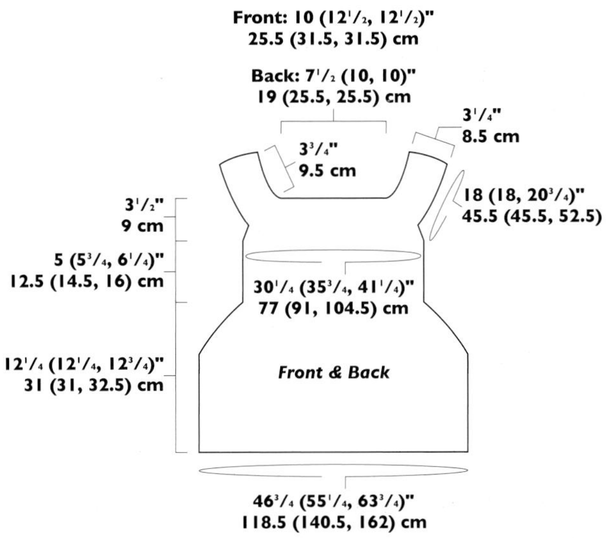

FIRST SHOULDER STRAP DEC RND: Work back sts in established patt to left strap sts, slip marker (sl m), *[k1, yo, k1, ssk, k1, sk2p, k1, k2tog, k1, yo] 3 times*, sl m, work front sts in established patt to right strap sts, sl m; rep from * to * once more—116 (132, 132) sts; 24 (32, 32) back sts; 32 (40, 40) front sts; 30 sts each shoulder strap.

Knit 1 rnd.

SECOND SHOULDER STRAP DEC RND: Work 24 (32, 32) back sts in established patt, sl m, *[k1, yo, k1, ssk, sk2p, k2tog, k1, yo] 3 times*, sl m, work 32 (40, 40) front sts in established patt, sl m; rep from * to * once more—104 (120, 120) sts; 24 (32, 32) back sts; 32 (40, 40) front sts; 24 sts each shoulder strap; all patt reps have been dec'd to 8 sts.

Knit 1 rnd. Work 4 rnds even in 8-st lace patt. Change to smallest needle. Knit 1 rnd, dec 8 (12, 12) sts evenly spaced—96 (108, 108) sts rem; piece measures 8½ (9¼, 9¾)″ (21.5 [23.5, 25] cm) from start of 8-st lace patt at underbust and 20¾ (21½, 22½)″ (52.5 [54.5, 57] cm) from CO at lower edge, measured straight up at center front or back; shoulder straps measure about 3¼″ (8.5 cm) above CO at underarms. With middle-size needle and using the decrease method (see Glossary), BO all sts.

Finishing

NECK EDGING

With RS facing, join CC to beg of back neck sts. Work crochet scallops (see Glossary for crochet instructions) as foll: Ch 1, *skip 2 sts, make 5-st shell by working 5 dc in next st, skip 2 sts, sc in next st; rep from * to end, join with a sl st to beg ch-1. Fasten off last st.

ARMHOLE EDGING

Return 16 (16, 24) held underarm sts to middle-size needle and join MC with RS facing. Insert crochet hook into first 2 sts, yo hook and draw through both sts, *insert crochet hook into next st, yo hook, and draw through both sts on hook; rep from * until all sts have been BO. Fasten off last st. Repeat for other underarm.

Weave in loose ends. Wet-block garment as recommended in Glossary, coaxing shoulder straps upward in a gentle curve to form a scooped neckline as shown on schematic.

Front: 10 (12½, 12½)″
25.5 (31.5, 31.5) cm

Back: 7½ (10, 10)″
19 (25.5, 25.5) cm

3¼″
8.5 cm

3¾″
9.5 cm

18 (18, 20¾)″
45.5 (45.5, 52.5)

3½″
9 cm

5 (5¾, 6¼)″
12.5 (14.5, 16) cm

30¼ (35¾, 41¼)″
77 (91, 104.5) cm

Front & Back

12¼ (12¼, 12¾)″
31 (31, 32.5) cm

46¾ (55¼, 63¾)″
118.5 (140.5, 162) cm

SOPHIA ✳ *cable-edged cardigan*

Although Italian in name, **Sophia wasn't inspired by a dramatic aria.** The design began more quietly. As the first garment I constructed with a newfound seamless method, this Chanel-style jacket came to represent a peaceful revolution for me. It pushed me toward creating more designs using seamless techniques.

I wanted to realign the normally horizontal classic stitch pattern called Roman Stripe in a body-enhancing manner yet also keep the sense of a single piece throughout the garment. Thereby began a lengthy knit-filled quest. The idea of constructing two body sections independently, then fashioning a joining graft to make them "one" appeared in the nick of time. It freed me from adding to the many orphan halves littering the French Girl studio!

Nubby wool/cotton organic yarn, usually reserved for more sporty designs, works against type here. It has just enough body to maintain the structure of the crochetlike openwork bodice and twisted garter edging, yet it has a soft hand when knitted and blocked.

FINISHED SIZE

32 (36, 40, 44, 48)" (81.5 [91.5, 101.5, 112, 122] cm) bust circumference; fronts do not meet in the middle. Sweater shown measures 32" (81.5 cm). NOTE: This garment may be worn with a narrower or wider gap at center front to accommodate smaller, larger, or in-between sizes.

YARN

DK weight (#3 Light).
SHOWN HERE: Vermont Organic Fiber Company O-Wool Balance (50% merino, 50% cotton; 130 yd [119 ml/50 g): #1000 natural, 6 (7, 8, 9, 10) skeins.

NEEDLES

BODY AND SLEEVES: size 6 (4 mm): straight, 16" and 36" (40 and 90 cm) circular (cir), and set of 4 or 5 double-pointed (dpn). EDGING AND SLEEVE CUFFS: size U.S. 5 (3.75 mm): 36" (90 cm) cir and set of 4 or 5 dpn. *Adjust needle size if necessary to obtain the correct gauge.*

NOTIONS

Marker (m); smooth cotton waste yarn for provisional cast-on; size G/7 (4.5 mm) crochet hook; stitch holders; tapestry needle.

GAUGE

13½ stitches and 24 rows/rounds = 4" (10 cm) in Roman stripe pattern on larger needles (see Note about counting stitches); 19 stitches = 4" (10 cm) wide in garter st on larger needles.

Notes

The garment is worked in two halves, each half beginning at the sleeve cuff and worked in the round to the top of the sleeve where stitches are cast on at each side for the back and front using the crochet-on method. The piece continues back and forth in rows to the neck edge where the front stitches are placed on hold. The back stitches are worked separately to the center back where a small triangular gusset is worked at the lower edge on one half. The two pieces are grafted together at the center back.

Because the stitch count of the Roman stripe pattern does not remain constant throughout, do not count stitches after having completed Rows/Rounds 1 and 2 when the stitch count has doubled from its original number. Unless otherwise specified, stitch counts given in the directions are after having completed Rows/Rounds 3-6 when the stitch count has been restored to its original number. When checking gauge, use the number of stitches cast-on or after completing Rows/Rounds 3-6.

The twisted garter st edging used for the front band is an adaptation of the Stockinette Stitch T Twist found in Nicky Epstein's *Knitting on the Edge*.

Stitch Guide

ROMAN STRIPE PATTERN IN ROUNDS

(EVEN NUMBER OF STS)

RND 1: *Yo, k1; rep from *.

RND 2: Knit.

RND 3: *K2tog; rep from*.

RND 4: *P2tog, yo; rep from * to last 2 sts, k2.

RND 5: *Yo, k2tog; rep from * to last 2 sts, k2.

RND 6: Knit into the back loop of the first st (yo at beg of previous rnd), knit to end.

Repeat Rnds 1–6 for pattern. NOTE: Stitch count increases after Rnd 1 and decreases back to original number after Rnd 3; be careful not to drop any yarnovers that fall at the ends of the needles.

ROMAN STRIPE PATTERN IN ROWS

(EVEN NUMBER OF STS)

ROW 1: (RS) K1, *yo, k1; rep from * to last st, k1.

ROW 2: K1, purl to last st, k1.

ROW 3: K1, *k2tog; rep from * to last st, k1.

ROWS 4 AND 5: K1, *yo, k2tog; rep from * to last st, k1.

ROW 6: Rep Row 2.

Repeat Rows 1–6 for pattern. NOTE: Stitch count increases after Row 1 and decreases back to original number after Row 3.

Right Half

SLEEVE

With smaller dpn and using the cable method (see Glossary), CO 50 (52, 56, 62, 68) sts. Place marker (pm) and join for working in rnds, being careful not to twist sts.

RND 1: *K1, p1; rep from *.

RND 2: *P1, k1; rep from *.

Rep Rnds 1 and 2 once more—4 rnds total; piece measures about ½" (1.3 cm) from CO. Change to larger dpn. Work Rnds 1–6 of Roman stripe patt in rnds (see Stitch Guide) 5 (5, 5, 6, 6) times, then work Rnds 1 and 2 of patt once more, temporarily transferring sts to shorter cir needle in larger size if there are too many sts to fit comfortably on dpns on the rnds when the st count increases—100 (104, 112, 124, 136) sts counted after completing Rnd 2.

INC RND: (Rnd 3 of patt) K4, *k2tog; rep from to last 4 sts, k4—54 (56, 60, 66, 72) sts.

Work Rnds 4–6 of patt, then work Rnds 1 and 2 once more—108 (112, 120, 132, 144) sts counted after completing Rnd 2. Rep the inc rnd once more—58 (60, 64, 70, 76) sts. Work Rnds 4–6 of patt—piece measures about 7½ (7½, 7½, 8½, 8½)" (19 [19, 19, 21.5, 21.5] cm) from CO.

FRONT AND BACK

Place sleeve sts on shorter cir needle in larger size. With crochet hook and smooth waste yarn, use the crochet-on method (see Glossary) to provisionally CO 31 (33, 35, 37, 39) right front sts onto straight needle in larger size. Join new yarn to beg of new CO sts with RS facing. Using longer cir needle in larger size, work Row 1 of Roman stripe patt in rows (see Stitch Guide) as foll: (RS) K1, [yo, k1] 29 (31, 33, 35, 37) times, yo, k2tog (last CO st tog with first sleeve st), [yo, k1] 56 (58, 62, 68, 74) times, set aside temporarily, leaving the last st unworked. Using straight needle in larger size and working from lower edge toward underarm, pick up 31 (33, 35, 37, 39) sts for right back from main yarn loops at base of provisional CO. With RS facing and using yarn attached at end of sleeve, cont as foll: Yo, k2tog (last sleeve st tog with first CO st), [yo, k1] 29 (31, 33, 35, 37) times, k1—234 (246, 262, 282, 302) sts after completing Row 1. NOTE: Because there are sts worked from both sides of the same provisional CO, the cable section of the cir needle will be folded in half in a tight hairpin bend; it will become easier to slide the sts around this bend as the work progresses.

NEXT ROW: (Row 2 of patt) K1, purl to last st, k1.

NEXT ROW: (Row 3 of patt) K1, *k2tog; rep from * to last st, k1—118 (124, 132, 142, 152) sts.

Work Rows 4–6 once, rep Rows 1–6 of patt 5 (6, 7, 8, 9) more times, then work Rows 1–5 once more, ending with a RS row—piece measures about 7 (8, 9, 10, 11)" (18 [20.5, 23, 25.5, 28] cm) from front and back CO, and about 14½ (15½, 16½, 18½, 19½)" (37 [39.5, 42, 47, 49.5] cm) from beg of sleeve. With RS facing, place first 68 (72, 76, 82, 88) sts on holder for right front and right side of back neck—50 (52, 56, 60, 64) back sts rem.

SHORT-ROW GUSSET

Work short-rows (see Glossary) as foll:

SHORT-ROW 1: (WS) K12, wrap next st, turn.

SHORT-ROWS 2, 4, 6, 8, AND 10: (RS) Knit to end. NOTE: Working wrapped sts tog with their wraps on the foll rows is optional because the garter-stitch fabric will conceal any holes at the turning points.

SHORT-ROWS 3, 5, 7, AND 9: Knit to previously wrapped st, work wrapped st either by itself or tog with its wrap, k1, wrap next st, turn—wrapped st of Short-row 9 is the 21st st from beg of row.

SHORT-ROWS 10, 12, 14, AND 16: Knit to end.

SHORT-ROW 11: K18, wrap next st, turn.

SHORT-ROWS 13, 15, AND 17: Knit to 3 sts before previously wrapped st, wrap next st, turn—wrapped st of Short-row 17 is the 13th st from beg of row.

7 (8, 9, 10, 11)"
18 (20.5, 23, 25.5, 28) cm

7½ (7½, 7½, 8½, 8½)"
19 (19, 19, 21.5, 21.5) cm

8½ (8¾, 9¼, 10¼, 11¼)"
21.5 (22, 23.5, 26, 28.5) cm

Right Half Back View

9 (9½, 10, 10¾, 11¼)"
23 (24, 25.5, 27.5, 28.5) cm

12 (12½, 13½, 14¾, 16¼)"
30.5 (31.5, 34.5, 37.5, 41.5) cm

SHORT-ROW 18: Knit to end—gusset measures about 3″ (7.5 cm) from last Roman stripe patt row at lower back edge (end of RS rows).

Knit 1 WS row across all sts, working rem wrapped sts tog with their wraps if desired. Place sts on holder.

Left Half

SLEEVE

Work as for right half—58 (60, 64, 70, 76) sts; piece measures about 7½ (7½, 7½, 8½, 8½)″ (19 [19, 19, 21.5, 21.5] cm) from CO.

FRONT AND BACK

Place sleeve sts on shorter cir needle in larger size. With crochet hook and smooth waste yarn, use the crochet-on method to CO 31 (33, 35, 37, 39) left back sts onto straight needle in larger size. Join new yarn to beg of new CO sts with RS facing. Using longer cir needle in larger size, work Row 1 of Roman stripe patt in rows as foll: (RS) K1, [yo, k1] 29 (31, 33, 35, 37) times, yo, k2tog (last CO st tog with first sleeve st), [yo, k1] 56 (58, 62, 68, 74) times, set aside temporarily, leaving 1 st unworked. Using straight needle in larger size and working from lower edge toward under-arm, pick up 31 (33, 35, 37, 39) sts for left front from main yarn loops at base of provisional CO sts. With RS facing and using yarn attached at end of sleeve, cont as foll: Yo, k2tog (last sleeve st tog with first CO st), [yo, k1] 29 (31, 33, 35, 37) times, k1—234 (246, 262, 282, 302) sts after completing Row 1.

NEXT ROW: (Row 2 of patt) K1, purl to last st, k1.

NEXT ROW: (Row 3 of patt) K1, *k2tog; rep from * to last st, k1—118 (124, 132, 142, 152) sts.

Work Rows 4–6 once, then rep Rows 1–6 of patt 6 (7, 8, 9, 10) more times, ending with a WS row—piece measures about 7 (8, 9, 10, 11)″ (18 [20.5, 23, 25.5, 28] cm) from front and back CO, and about 14½ (15½, 16½, 18½, 19½)″ (37 [39.5, 42, 47, 49.5] cm) from beg of sleeve. With RS facing, place first 50 (52, 56, 60, 64) sts on holder for back, then place rem 68 (72, 76, 82, 88) sts on holder for left front and left side of back neck. NOTE: Left half does not include short-row gusset shown on schematic for right half. With yarn threaded on a tapestry needle, use the Kitchener st (see Glossary) to graft the 50 (52, 56, 60, 64) sts of the right and left backs tog. Block to finished measurements.

Finishing

NECK EDGING

With RS facing, join yarn to end of held right half sts at back neck. Stretch back neck area between the two groups of held sts as necessary, and using crochet hook, work 14 single crochet sts (sc; see Glossary) from end of right half held sts to beg of left half held sts, working more than 1 sc into each openwork space as required. Fasten off last st and break yarn. Place 68 (72, 76, 82, 88) held sts of both right and left halves on smaller cir needle—136 (144, 152, 164, 176) sts. Join yarn with RS facing to lower right front corner.

NEXT ROW: (RS) K68 (72, 76, 82, 88) right half sts, place marker (pm), pick up and knit 1 st in each of 14 sc at back neck, pm, k68 (72, 76, 82, 88) left half sts—150 (158, 166, 178, 190) sts.

Knit 1 WS row. Set aside.

With longer cir needle in larger size and using the long-tail method (see Glossary), CO 232 (244, 256, 274, 292) sts. Slipping the first st of every row pwise wyb, work in garter st for 15 rows, beg and ending with a WS row.

NEXT ROW: (RS) K 1 (2, 3, 2, 1), *K10, bring the point of the left needle down in front of the work, underneath the CO edge, and up in back of the work to twist the piece one complete 360-degree turn between the needles; rep from * to last 11 (12, 13, 12, 11) sts, k11 (12, 13, 12, 11).

Slipping the first st of every row, work 8 more rows even in garter st, ending with a RS row. Leave sts on needle and do not break yarn. Hold needles with live sts of body and twisted garter edging parallel with garter edging in front, RS of both pieces facing tog, and WS facing out. Using the yarn attached to the twisted garter edging, use a modified three-needle bind-off to join live sts of edging and body tog as foll: Insert right needle tip into first st on edging needle, then into first st on body needle, and knit these 2 sts tog as 1 st, *insert right needle tip into first 2 sts on edging needle, then into next st on body needle, and knit all 3 sts tog as 1 st, pass first st on right needle over second st to BO 1, insert right needle tip into first st on edging needle, then into first st on body needle, and knit these 2 sts tog as 1 st, pass first st on right needle over second st to BO 1;* rep from * to * 32 (34, 36, 39, 42) more times, alternating joining sts 1-to-1 and 2-to-1, and ending 1 st before marked back neck sts—67 (71, 75, 81, 87) right half sts joined to 100 (106, 112, 121, 130) twisted edging sts. Join next 15 body sts to next 30 twisted edging sts

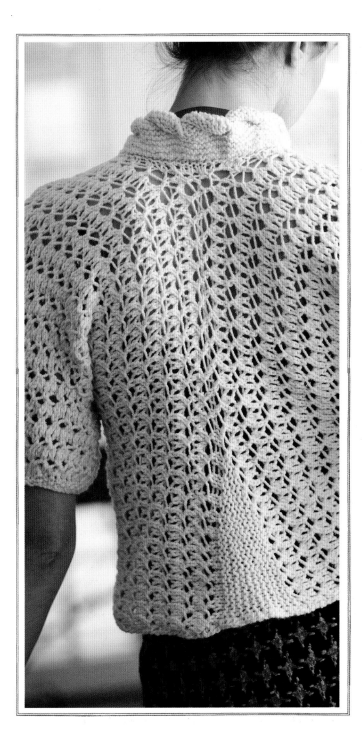

by joining 2 edging sts to 1 body st 15 times—82 (86, 90, 96, 102) total body sts joined to 130 (136, 142, 151, 160) total twisted edging sts. Join rem 68 (72, 76, 82, 88) left half body sts to rem 102 (108, 114, 123, 132) twisted edging sts by working from * to * 34 (36, 38, 41, 44) times. Fasten off last st. With yarn threaded on tapestry needle, invisibly tack down the scalloped twists at the lower edge of each front, twisting them to match the curves of the other scallops.

LOWER EDGING

With RS facing, join yarn to lower corner of left front at the row between the plain and twisted sections of the neck edging. With longer cir needle in larger size, pick up and knit sts around lower edge of body as foll (about 4 sts for every 6 rows of Roman stripe patt or 4 garter ridges of twisted edging): 32 (36, 40, 44, 48) sts to left side "seam," 28 (32, 36, 40, 44) sts along left back to gusset, 14 sts across gusset selvedge, 28 (32, 36, 40, 44) sts to right side "seam," and 32 (36, 40, 44, 48) sts to row between plain and twisted sections of neck edging—134 (150, 166, 182, 198) sts total. With WS facing and using the decrease method (see Glossary), BO all sts.

Weave in loose ends. Lightly block again, if desired.

SIDE-TO-SIDE
SEAMLESS CONSTRUCTION

When I began work on *French Girl Knits*, I wanted to experiment with as many construction methods as possible, exploring their potential to be reimagined seamlessly. Most traditional side-to-side garments are created flat. You begin knitting at one cuff, then work up the sleeve to the armhole, where you cast on additional stitches for the front and back. You work the front and back simultaneously to the neck. The two are split for the width of the neck opening, then rejoined and worked simultaneously to the other armhole. You bind off the stitches and work the other sleeve down to the cuff. After all that knitting, you have two very long seams to sew or graft along the sides and sleeves.

Thankfully, you have a seamless option, which in its most basic cardigan application involves only one seam to be grafted along the center back of the garment. (A pullover would involve an additional grafted seam along the center front if the patterns are to match on each side.) Other than reducing the finishing step to a single seam (or two), the circular method makes it easier to align stitch patterns and allows for custom fitting along the way. The designs worked in this manner are Sophia (page 14), Celeste (page 92), and Bijou (page 140).

FIGURE 1

You construct this type of sweater in two halves, beginning at the cuff edge of one sleeve. You work the first sleeve in rounds using increases or decreases to taper the sleeve and curve the underarms (Figure 1). If necessary, you can work short-rows to shape the sleeve cap. When the sleeve is the desired length (see Knit to Fit, page 53), you use a provisional method to cast on stitches onto a separate needle for one side of the side seam (Figure 2). You work across the provisionally cast-on stitches, then across the existing sleeve stitches (Figure 3). You then pick up the loops from the provisionally cast-on stitches (see box on page 23) for the other side of the side seam (Figure 4), and voilà—you have just "sewn" the first side seam!

TIPS FOR SIDE-TO-SIDE CONSTRUCTION

- Practice this method on a sample with smooth worsted-weight yarn before attempting a full-size garment. Cast on enough stitches to work circularly on a 16″ (40 cm) needle, knit for about 2″ (5 cm) to approximate the sleeve, then cast on enough stitches to create a miniature side seam. Work back and forth for an inch or two to become comfortable with the technique.

- Clearly mark the right and left sleeves to avoid confusion in the early stages, especially if you work on both halves of the garment at the same time.

- Be sure to use long circular needles for the joining row. They are paramount for this method, especially when they finesse the fit after you join the body and sleeves.

- To fit the sleeve correctly, remember that blocking and joining the bodice and sleeves will add length. Adjust accordingly based on your own measurements and your blocked swatch.

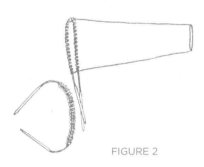

FIGURE 2

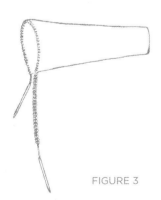

FIGURE 3

FIGURE 4

Take a moment at this point to check the number and mount of the picked-up stitches. It's easy to inadvertently pick up some stitches backward or to lose one or two at either end of the cast-on. From this point on, the work progresses back and forth in long rows that extend from the back hem over the top of the shoulder and down to the front hem (Figure 5) to the beginning of the neck shaping, with body shaping worked along the way. You can work this part on a single very long circular needle or on two shorter circular needles. I prefer to use two circular needles that are long enough to let me stretch the knitting to its full length, so I can fine-tune the fit as I go. To allow for the neck opening, you work the stitches for the front and back separately to the center front and center back (Figure 6). You can then set this piece aside and make another half to match, reversing the shaping for the front and back.

Use the Kitchener stitch (see Glossary) to graft the two pieces together "seamlessly"—along the center back and center front for a pullover or along just the center back for a cardigan. To finish, add edgings as desired.

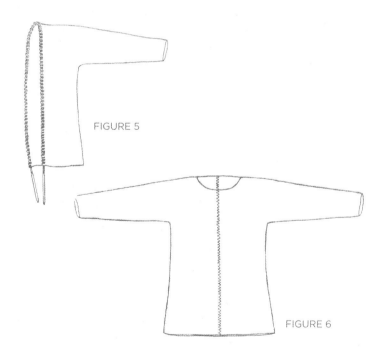

FIGURE 5

FIGURE 6

PICKING UP STITCHES FROM A PROVISIONAL CAST-ON

I like to use one of two methods to pick up stitches from a provisional cast-on, depending on the type of yarn I've chosen.

WITH WASTE YARN IN PLACE

This method is particularly useful with slippery or sticky yarns, such as silk or mohair. With the waste yarn still in place, lift each cast-on loop onto a circular needle two or three sizes smaller than the size used for knitting (Figure 1). When all of the loops have been lifted onto the needle, remove the waste yarn. Begin knitting with the proper-size needle.

AS WASTE YARN IS REMOVED

This method works best with yarns such as wool that hold the shape of the stitches when the needles are removed. Using a needle the same size as the one used for knitting, place each exposed cast-on stitch on the needle as you remove the waste yarn (Figure 2).

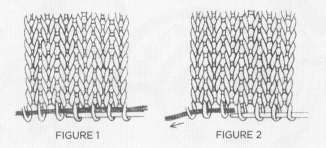

FIGURE 1   FIGURE 2

ANJOU ✳ *lacy tie-hem tunic*

Gabrielle Chanel, or "Coco," as she came to be called, was my secret guide for Anjou, although I arrived at that realization long after the design was completed. We associate Chanel with the "little black dress," crisp, stripped-down jackets, and the iconic double-C logo gracing some of fashion's most spendy items. Perusing a retrospective of her early work, including evocative handpainted renditions of gowns from the 1920s and 1930s, I discovered a soft pear-green lace design with a double-layered hem that could have been Anjou in another life. Had I been channeling Chanel? Oh, to be so fortunate!

Coco Chanel's life story continues to inspire us: orphaned at twelve, she became a designer who defied convention with her corsetless, unpredictable creations. She went on to reinvent modern women's couture with a look that's timeless.

The magical yarn that made this garment work is a blend of linen and merino, which creates a fabric with tonality and drape. The lace dripping from hem and sleeve depends on that drape to achieve the languorous, vintage look I was seeking.

FINISHED SIZE

30 (32½, 35¾, 38¼, 41¼)" (76.5 [82.5, 91, 97, 104.5] cm) bust circumference. Tunic shown measures 30" (76 cm). NOTE: This garment is designed with about 3" (7.5 cm) negative wearing ease for a close, body-conscious fit.

YARN

Laceweight (#0 Lace).
SHOWN HERE: Louet KidLin Lace Weight (49% linen, 35% kid mohair, 16% nylon; 250 yd [229 ml/50 g): #41 woodland, 4 (4, 4, 5, 5) skeins.

NEEDLES

BODY, HIP BAND, AND SLEEVES: size U.S. 9 (5.5 mm): 16", 24", and 36" (40, 60, and 90 cm) circular (cir). YOKE: size U.S. 8 (5 mm): 16", 24", and 36" (40, 60, and 90 cm) cir. *Adjust needle size if necessary to obtain the correct gauge.*

NOTIONS

Markers (m); stitch holders; smooth cotton waste yarn for provisional cast-on; removable markers; tapestry needle.

GAUGE

15½ stitches and 25 rows/rounds = 4" (10 cm) in stockinette using larger needle; 24 stitches (at widest point) and 40 rows (4 patt reps) of sleeve patterns measure 7½" (19 cm) wide and 7" (18 cm) high on larger needle, after blocking. See Notes for lace gauge swatch suggestion.

Notes

- The beginning of one sleeve can be used as a lace gauge swatch. Cast on 20 stitches and work the sleeve pattern for 4" to 5" (10 to 12.5 cm), then place the stitches on a length of waste yarn and block. If the gauge is correct, continue with the sleeve. If not, change needle size and start again.
- The yoke is worked in the round in one piece from the neck edge down. Stitches are placed on holders for the armholes. The upper front and back are worked separately back and forth for a different number of rows to the underarms to create a lower neckline in front than in back. The front and back are then rejoined and worked in the round to the lower edge where the stitches are placed on holders.
- The lace hip band is worked in two pieces that are grafted together with the join at center back so the diagonals of the lace patterns in the ties are mirror images.
- Stitches are picked up along one selvedge of the completed hip band and grafted to the live stitches of the lower body. The lace sleeves are worked separately back and forth in rows, then grafted to armholes in a similar manner.
- For the hip band and sleeves, slip the first stitch of all RS rows as if to purl with yarn in back, and slip the first stitch of all WS rows as if to purl with yarn in front.
- The hip band and sleeves are not shown on the schematic.

Stitch Guide

KRB
Knit into st in the row below the next st on left needle—1 st inc'd.

PRB
Purl into st in the row below the next st on left needle—1 st inc'd.

Yoke

With smaller size 24" (60 cm) cir needle, CO 72 sts very loosely. Place marker (pm) and join for working in rnds, being careful not to twist sts; rnd begs at center back.

RNDS 1 AND 2: *K1, p1; rep from *.

RND 3: *Krb (see Stitch Guide), k1, p1; rep from *—108 sts.

RND 4: Work according to your size as foll:

SIZE 30" ONLY

Knit the knits and purl the purls as they appear.

SIZE 32¹/₂" ONLY

*Work 9 sts in patt, work krb or prb (see Stitch Guide) to match next st on left needle; rep from *—120 sts.

SIZE 35³/₄" ONLY

*Work 4 sts in patt, work krb or prb (see Stitch Guide) to match next st on left needle, work 5 sts in patt, work krb or prb to match next st on left needle; rep from *—132 sts.

SIZE 38¹/₄" ONLY

*Work 3 sts in patt, work krb or prb (see Stitch Guide) to match next st on left needle; rep from *—144 sts.

SIZE 41¹/₄" ONLY

*Work 3 sts in patt, work krb or prb (see Stitch Guide) to match

next st on left needle, [work 2 sts in patt, work krb or prb to match next st] 3 times; rep from *—156 sts.

ALL SIZES

RNDS 5, 7, 9, 11, 13, AND 15: Knit.

RND 6: *K1, yo, k5, yo; rep from *—144 (160, 176, 192, 208) sts. NOTE: Change to longer cir needle in smaller size when necessary and be careful not to drop any yo's that occur at the end of a rnd.

RND 8: *K2, yo, ssk, k1, k2tog, yo, k1; rep from *.

RND 10: *K1, yo, k2, yo, sssk (see Glossary), yo, k2, yo; rep from *—180 (200, 220, 240, 260) sts.

RND 12: *K2, yo, ssk, k1, yo, ssk, k2tog, yo, k1; rep from *

RND 14: *K3, yo, ssk, k1, k2tog, yo, k2; rep from *.

RND 16: *K4, yo, sssk, yo, k3; rep from *.

RND 17: Knit—piece measures about 2³/₄" (7 cm) from CO. Cut yarn.

DIVIDE FRONT, BACK, AND ARMHOLES

With larger size 24" (60 cm) cir needle, sl first 19 (21, 24, 26, 29) sts of left back pwise without working any sts, place the next 42 (47, 51, 56, 60) sts on holder for left armhole, place next 59 (65, 71, 77, 83) sts on separate holder for front, place next 42 (47, 51, 56, 60) sts on another holder for right armhole, sl rem 18 (20, 23, 25, 28) sts pwise without working any sts for right back—37 (41, 47, 51, 57) back sts on larger needle. Cut yarn.

UPPER BACK

Rejoin yarn to back sts with WS facing. Work 17 (19, 21, 23, 25) rows even in St st, beg and ending with a WS row—piece measures about 5¹/₂ (5³/₄, 6, 6¹/₂, 6³/₄)" (14 [14.5, 15, 16.5, 17] cm) from CO.

INC ROW: (RS) Krb, knit to last st, krb—2 sts inc'd.

*Work 3 rows even in St st, rep inc row. Rep from * once more, then work 3 rows even—43 (47, 53, 57, 63) sts; piece measures about 7¹/₄ (7³/₄, 8, 8¹/₄, 8³/₄)" (18.5 [19.5, 20.5, 21, 22] cm) from CO. Place sts on holder.

UPPER FRONT

Place 59 (65, 71, 77, 83) held front sts on larger size 24" (60 cm) cir needle and rejoin yarn with WS facing. Work 3 (5, 7, 9, 11) rows even in St st, beg and ending with a WS row.

17"
43 cm

3¹/₂"
9 cm

3³/₄ (4¹/₄, 4¹/₂, 4³/₄, 5¹/₄)"
9.5 (11, 11.5, 12, 13.5) cm

13"
33 cm

Front & Back

30 (32¹/₂, 35³/₄, 38¹/₄, 41¹/₄)"
76 (82.5, 91, 97, 104.5) cm

34 (36¹/₂, 39³/₄, 42¹/₄, 45¹/₂)"
86.5 (92.5, 101, 107.5, 115.5) cm

INC ROW: (RS) Krb, knit to last st, krb—61 (67, 73, 79, 85) sts.

Work 3 rows even, ending with a WS row—piece measures about 3¾ (4¼, 4½, 4¾, 5¼)" (9.5 [11, 11.5, 12, 13.5] cm) from CO. Leave sts on needle.

Lower Body

Changing to 36" (90 cm) larger size cir needle if necessary, knit to end of 61 (67, 73, 79, 85) front sts, use the backward-loop method (see Glossary) to CO 1 st, pm for left side, CO 1 st, knit across 43 (47, 53, 57, 63) held back sts, CO 1 st, pm for right side, CO 1 st (counts as first st of next rnd)—108 (118, 130, 140, 152) sts total; 63 (69, 75, 81, 87) front sts; 45 (49, 55, 59, 65) back sts; rnd begs at right side. Knit to end of current rnd, then work 9 more rnds even—piece measures about 1¾" (4.5 cm) from joining rnd.

BUST INC RND: *K1, krb, knit to 1 st before m, krb, k1, slip marker (sl m); rep from * once more—4 sts inc'd, 2 sts each on front and back.

Work 3 rnds even in St st, then rep the inc rnd once more—116 (126, 138, 148, 160) sts; 67 (73, 79, 85, 91) front sts; 49 (53, 59, 63, 69) back sts. Work even in St st until piece measures 6½" (16.5 cm) from joining rnd.

WAIST DEC RND: *K2tog, knit to 2 sts before m, ssk, sl m; rep from * once more—4 sts dec'd, 2 sts each on front and back.

Work 1 rnd even, then rep waist dec rnd once more—108 (118, 130, 140, 152) sts; 63 (69, 75, 81, 87) front sts; 45 (49, 55, 59, 65) back sts. Work even until piece measures 7¾" (19.5 cm) from joining rnd.

HIP INC RND: *K1, krb, knit to 1 st before m, krb, k1, sl m; rep from * once more—4 sts inc'd, 2 sts each on front and back.

*Work 3 rnds even, then work hip inc rnd. Rep from * 4 more times—132 (142, 154, 164, 176) sts; 75 (81, 87, 93, 99) front sts; 57 (61, 67, 71, 77) back sts. Work even in St st until piece measures 13" (33 cm) from joining rnd or about 9½" (24 cm) less than desired total length, removing left side m on last rnd. Cut yarn. Sl first 65 (70, 76, 81, 87) front sts pwise without working them, then place a removable marker in the fabric between the two needle tips to indicate where the hip band attachment begins and ends; the hip band ties will be offset 10 (11, 11, 12, 12) sts to the front from the position of the original left side m. Leave sts on needle.

Sleeves

You may find it helpful to mark each sleeve as right or left as it is completed.

RIGHT SLEEVE

With larger size 24" (60 cm) cir needle and using a provisional method (see Glossary), CO 20 sts.

ROW 1: (RS) Sl 1 (see Notes), k1, yo, [k2tog, yo] 7 times, k4—21 sts.

ROWS 2, 4, 6, AND 8: (WS) Sl 1, purl to end.

ROW 3: Sl 1, k1, yo, [k2tog, yo] 6 times, k7—22 sts.

ROW 5: Sl 1, k1, yo, [k2tog, yo] 5 times, k10—23 sts.

ROW 7: Sl 1, k1, yo, [k2tog, yo] 4 times, k13—24 sts.

ROW 9: BO 4 sts (1 st on right needle after last BO), k19—20 sts rem.

ROW 10: Sl 1, p19.

Rep Rows 1-10 of patt 8 (9, 9, 10, 10) more times, then work Rows 1-8 once more—24 sts.

NEXT ROW: (RS; counts as Row 9 of patt) BO 14 sts, knit to end—10 sts rem.

NEXT ROW: (WS; counts as Row 10 of patt) Sl 1, purl to end—100 (110, 110, 120, 120) rows total.

Place sts on holder. Carefully remove waste yarn from provisional CO and place 20 exposed sts on shorter cir needle in larger size. Join yarn with WS facing at pointed selvedge and BO 10 sts—10 sts rem. Cut yarn, leaving a long tail for grafting. Thread tail on a tapestry needle and use the Kitchener st (see Glossary) to graft 10 sts from base of CO to 10 live sts on holder to join sleeve into a tube.

LEFT SLEEVE

With larger size 24" (60 cm) cir needle and using a provisional method, CO 20 sts.

ROW 1: (RS) Sl 1, k3, [yo, k2tog] 7 times, yo, k2—21 sts.

ROWS 2, 4, 6, AND 8: (WS) Sl 1, purl to end.

ROW 3: Sl 1, k6, [yo, k2tog] 6 times, yo, k2—22 sts.

ROW 5: Sl 1, k9, [yo, k2tog] 5 times, yo, k2—23 sts.

ROW 7: Sl 1, k12, [yo, k2tog] 4 times, yo, k2—24 sts.

ROW 9: Sl 1, k23.

ROW 10: BO 4 sts (1 st on right needle after last BO), p19—20 sts rem.

Rep Rows 1–10 of patt 8 (9, 9, 10, 10) more times, then work Rows 1–9 once more—24 sts.

NEXT ROW: (WS; counts as Row 10 of patt) BO 14 sts, knit to end—10 sts rem; 100 (110, 110, 120, 120) rows total.

Place sts on holder. Carefully remove waste yarn from provisional CO and place 20 exposed sts on shorter cir needle in larger size. Join yarn with RS facing at pointed selvedge and BO 10 sts—10 sts rem. Use the Kitchener st to graft ends of sleeve tog as for right sleeve.

Hip Band

LEFT BACK

With larger size 24" (60 cm) cir needle and using a provisional method, CO 24 sts.

ROW 1: (RS) Sl 1, k3, [yo, k2tog] 9 times, yo, k2—25 sts.

ROWS 2, 4, 6, 8, 10, AND 12: (WS) Sl 1, purl to end.

ROW 3: Sl 1, k6, [yo, k2tog] 8 times, yo, k2—26 sts.

ROW 5: Sl 1, k9, [yo, k2tog] 7 times, yo, k2—27 sts.

ROW 7: Sl 1, k12, [yo, k2tog] 6 times, yo, k2—28 sts.

ROW 9: Sl 1, k15, [yo, k2tog] 5 times, yo, k2—29 sts.

ROW 11: Sl 1, k18, [yo, k2tog] 4 times, yo, k2—30 sts.

ROW 13: Sl 1, k29.

ROW 14: BO 6 sts (1 st rem on right needle after last BO), p23—24 sts rem.

Rep Rows 1–14 of patt 9 (10, 10, 11, 11) more times, placing a removable marker in the fabric at beg of Row 3 in the 5 (6, 6, 7, 7)th rep, 59 (73, 73, 87, 87) rows from beg, to mark location for picking up sts later—140 (154, 154, 168, 168) rows total. Loosely BO all sts.

RIGHT BACK AND FRONT

Carefully remove waste yarn from provisional CO and place 24 exposed sts plus 1 extra picked-up loop from CO edge on larger size 24" (60 cm) cir needle—25 sts. Join yarn with WS facing. NOTE: For the first rep only, skip directly to Row 2 and beg the patt with WS Row 2; for all foll reps, work all 14 rows of patt.

ROW 1: (RS; do not work for first rep) Sl 1, k1, yo, [k2tog, yo] 9 times, k4—25 sts.

ROWS 2, 4, 6, 8, 10, AND 12: (WS) Sl 1, purl to end.

ROW 3: Sl 1, k1, yo, [k2tog, yo] 8 times, k7—26 sts.

ROW 5: Sl 1, k1, yo, [k2tog, yo] 7 times, k10—27 sts.

ROW 7: Sl 1, k1, yo, [k2tog, yo] 6 times, k13—28 sts.

ROW 9: Sl 1, k1, yo, [k2tog, yo] 5 times, k16—29 sts.

ROW 11: Sl 1 pwise, k1, yo, [k2tog, yo] 4 times, k19—30 sts.

ROW 13: BO 6 sts (1 st rem on right needle after last BO), k23—24 sts rem.

ROW 14: Sl 1, p23.

Rep Rows 1–14 of patt 15 (16, 16, 17, 17) more times, placing a removable marker in the fabric at end of Row 2 in the 11 (12, 12, 13, 13)th rep, 142 (156, 156, 170, 170) rows from beg of this section, to mark location for picking up sts later—223 (237, 237, 251, 251) rows in this section of band; 363 (391, 391, 419, 419) rows total for both sections tog. Loosely BO all sts. Markers are 81 rows from each end of completed band with 201 (229, 229, 257, 257) rows or about 100 (114, 114, 128, 128) slipped edge sts between them.

Finishing

Transfer held armhole and lower edge sts to waste yarn and block body lightly to measurements, coaxing armhole sections of yoke upward in a gentle curve to form a scooped neckline as shown on schematic. Block sleeves (not shown on schematic) to about 17½ (19½, 19½, 21, 21)" (44.5 [49.5, 49.5, 53.5, 53.5] cm) around or 8¾ (9¾, 9¾, 10½, 10½)" (22 [25, 25, 26.5, 26.5] cm) tall when laid flat, and 7½" (19 cm) wide from straight selvedge to deepest point, pinning out each point. Block hip band (not shown on schematic) in the same manner to about 63½ (68½, 68½, 73¼, 73¼)" (161.5 [174, 174, 186, 186] cm) long and 9½" (24 cm) wide at deepest point.

JOIN HIP BAND TO LOWER BODY

Hold hip band and lower body tog so that right back and front piece is on the right-hand side, and selvedge with marked sts is at top. Join yarn with RS facing to m on right back and front piece. With smaller 36" (90 cm) cir needle and RS facing, pick up and knit 132 (142, 154, 164, 176) sts evenly between markers along selvedge of hip band (about 4 [5, 4, 5, 4] sts for every 3 [4, 3, 4, 3] slipped selvedge sts); the 81 rows on each side of the picked-up section will become the ties for the hip band. Cut yarn, leaving a long tail for grafting. With tail threaded on a tapestry needle, use the Kitchener st to graft picked-up sts to 132 (142, 154, 164, 176) live sts at lower edge of body, beg and ending at marked position on lower body 10 (11, 11, 12, 12) sts forward from the location of the original left side m.

JOIN SLEEVES TO ARMHOLES

Right Sleeve

Join yarn with RS facing to straight selvedge of right sleeve at grafted sleeve "seam." With larger 16" (40 cm) cir needle and RS facing, pick up and knit 60 (70, 80, 90, 90) sts around top of sleeve (about 6 to 7 sts for every 5 slipped selvedge sts). Cut yarn, leaving a long tail for grafting. Place 42 (47, 51, 56, 60) held sts of right armhole on smaller 16" (40 cm) cir needle. With RS of garment facing, join yarn to end of live armhole sts, then pick up and knit 4 (5, 7, 8, 9) sts along selvedge of upper right front, 2 sts from CO sts at base armhole, and 17 (18, 19, 20, 21) sts along selvedge of upper right back, then knit across 42 (47, 51, 56, 60) sts to end—65 (72, 79, 86, 92) sts total. Knit 1 rnd, dec 5 (dec 2, inc 1, inc 4, dec 2) st(s) evenly spaced—60 (70, 80, 90, 90) sts. With tail from sleeve pick-up threaded on a tapestry needle, use the Kitchener st to graft sleeve and armhole sts tog.

Left Sleeve

With larger 16" (40 cm) cir needle, pick up and knit 60 (70, 80, 90, 90) sts along straight selvedge at top of left sleeve as for right sleeve. Cut yarn, leaving a long tail for grafting. Place 42 (47, 51, 56, 60) held sts of left armhole on smaller 16" (40 cm) cir needle. With RS of garment facing, join yarn to end of live armhole sts, then pick up and knit 17 (18, 19, 20, 21) sts along selvedge of upper left back, 2 sts from CO sts at base armhole, and 4 (5, 7, 8, 9) sts along selvedge of upper left front, then knit across 42 (47, 51, 56, 60) sts to end—65 (72, 79, 86, 92) sts total. Knit 1 rnd, dec 5 (dec 2, inc 1, inc 4, dec 2) st(s) evenly spaced—60 (70, 80, 90, 90) sts. Graft sleeve and armhole sts tog as for right sleeve.

Weave in loose ends. To wear, tie ends of hip band.

ANJOU

PALOMA ✳ *cap-sleeve blouse*

FINISHED SIZE

33¼ (35½, 40, 42¼, 46¾)" (84.5 [90, 101.5, 107.5, 118.5] cm) bust circumference. Sweater shown measures 33¼" (84.5 cm).

YARN

Sportweight (#2 Fine).
SHOWN HERE: Louet MerLin Sport-weight (60% linen, 40% merino; 250 yd [229 ml/100 g): #21 cloud gray, 2 (3, 3, 4, 4) skeins.

NEEDLES

YOKE, UPPER BODY, AND SLEEVE EDG-INGS: size U.S. 3 (3.25 mm): 24" (60 cm) circular (cir) and set of 4 or 5 double-pointed (dpn). LOWER BODY: sizes U.S. 4 and 5 (3.5 and 3.75 mm): 24" (60 cm) cir. *Adjust needle size if necessary to obtain the correct gauge.*

NOTIONS

Stitch holders; markers (m); removable marker or safety pin; tapestry needle; strip of silk gauze fabric about 2½" (6.5 cm) wide and 72" (183 cm) long for neckline tie.

GAUGE

18 stitches and 26 rounds = 4" (10 cm) in granite rib pattern on size 3 (3.25 mm) needle; 16 stitches and 32 rounds = 4" (10 cm) in 13-stitch scallop pattern on size 4 (3.5 mm) needle; 14½ stitches and 30 rounds = 4" (10 cm) in 15-stitch scallop pattern on size 5 (3.75 mm) needle.

Pablo Picasso and his new amour, artist Françoise Gilot, decamped from post-war Paris to Vallaruis in the South of France: There, his compound became a magnet for artists, reeling in the likes of Henri Matisse, Marc Chagall, and Jean Cocteau. Françoise, one of the few women in the throng, has always intrigued me for her determination to retain her own painterly voice amid the rabble. Gilot's slice-of-life memoir, *Life with Picasso*, bears captivating witness to this fascinating time and place.

Not surprisingly, Françoise is creative on many fronts, and her daughter Paloma Picasso is equally gifted. Paloma seemed a perfect name for this dove-gray linen and merino garment that had one foot in a stylish Parisian world and the other in freewheeling bohemia. The circularly knitted lace upper bodice gives way to a swirling reinterpretation of the feather-and-fan pattern on the drop-stitch, biasing lower section. Add the slightly deconstructed silk fabric ribbon at the neckline for a touch of Beat-generation chic.

Notes

- The yoke is worked in the round in one piece from the neck down to the underarms where stitches are put on holders for the cap sleeves, then the front and back are worked in the round in one piece to the lower edge. The cap sleeve edgings are worked in the round from the underarms.
- The scallop patterns in the lower body naturally bias to create the spiral effect shown.

Stitch Guide

PRB

Purl into st in the row below the next st on left needle—1 st inc'd.

KRB

Knit into st in the row below the next st on left needle—1 st inc'd.

GRANITE RIB STITCH *(MULTIPLE OF 5 STS)*

RND 1: *P1, [k2tog, yo] 2 times; rep from *.

RND 2: *K1, [yo, k2tog tbl] 2 times; rep from *.

Repeat Rnds 1 and 2 for pattern.

13-STITCH SCALLOP PATTERN *(MULTIPLE OF 13 STS)*

RND 1: *[Ssk] 2 times, [k2tog] 2 times, [k1, yo] 4 times, k1; rep from *.

RND 2: Knit.

RND 3: Purl.

RND 4: *[K1, yo] 13 times; rep from *—patt rep has inc'd to a multiple of 26 sts. Be careful not to drop the yo at end of rnd.

RND 5: Knit, dropping each yo as you come to it to create a rnd of deliberately elongated sts—patt rep has dec'd back to a multiple of 13 sts.

RND 6: Knit.

RND 7: Purl.

RND 8: Knit.

Repeat Rnds 1–8 for pattern.

14-STITCH SCALLOP PATTERN *(MULTIPLE OF 14 STS)*

RND 1: *[Ssk] 2 times, k1, [k2tog] 2 times, [k1, yo] 4 times, k1; rep from *.

RNDS 2 AND 3: Work as for 13-st scallop.

RND 4: *[K1, yo] 14 times; rep from *—patt rep has inc'd to a multiple of 28 sts.

RND 5: Knit, dropping each yo as you come to it to create a rnd of deliberately elongated sts—patt rep has dec'd back to a multiple of 14 sts.

RNDS 6-8: Work as for 13-st scallop.

Repeat Rnds 1–8 for pattern.

15-STITCH SCALLOP PATTERN *(MULTIPLE OF 15 STS)*

RND 1: *[Ssk] 2 times, k2, [k2tog] 2 times, [k1, yo] 4 times, k1; rep from *.

RNDS 2 AND 3: Work as for 13-st scallop.

RND 4: *[K1, yo] 15 times; rep from *—patt rep has inc'd to a multiple of 30 sts.

RND 5: Knit, dropping each yo as you come to it to create a rnd of deliberately elongated sts—patt rep has dec'd back to a multiple of 15 sts.

RNDS 6-8: Work as for 13-st scallop.

Repeat Rnds 1–8 for pattern.

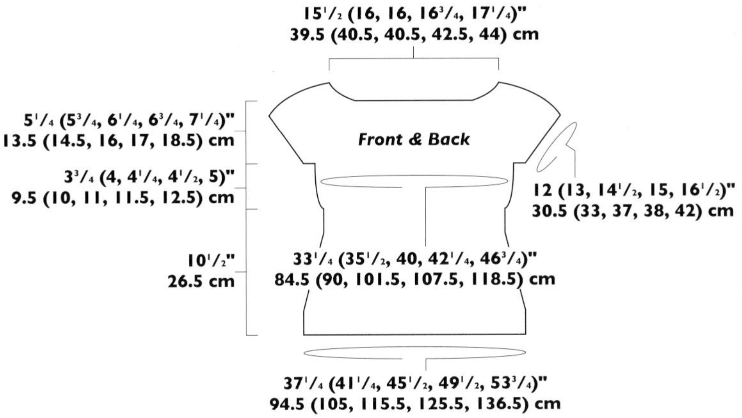

Yoke

With size 3 (3.25 mm) cir needle and using the long-tail method (see Glossary), CO 122 (126, 126, 132, 136) sts. Place marker (pm) and join for working in rnds, being careful not to twist sts. Purl 1 rnd.

EYELET RND: *K2tog, yo; rep from *.

NEXT RND: Using the prb method (see Stitch Guide), inc 3 (9, 29, 33, 49) sts evenly spaced—125 (135, 155, 165, 185) sts.

Cont as foll:

RND 1: *K1, [yo, k2togtbl (see Glossary)] 2 times; rep from *.

RND 2: *P1, [k2tog, yo] 2 times; rep from *.

RND 3: *Prb, k1, [yo, k2togtbl] 2 times; rep from *—150 (162, 186, 198, 222) sts.

RNDS 4, 6, AND 8: *K1, p1, [k2tog, yo] 2 times; rep from *.

RNDS 5 AND 7: *P1, k1, [yo, k2togtbl] 2 times; rep from *.

RND 9: *K1, prb, k1, [yo, k2togtbl] 2 times; rep from *—175 (189, 217, 231, 259) sts.

RNDS 10, 12, and 14: *P1, k1, p1, [k2tog, yo] 2 times; rep from *.

RNDS 11 AND 13: *K1, p1, k1, [yo, k2togtbl] 2 times; rep from *.

RND 15: *K1, p1, krb, p1, [yo, k2togtbl] 2 times; rep from *—200 (216, 248, 264, 296) sts.

RNDS 16, 18, 20, and 22: *[P1, k1] 2 times, [k2tog, yo] 2 times; rep from *.

RNDS 17, 19, AND 21: *[K1, p1] 2 times, [yo, k2togtbl] 2 times; rep from *.

RND 23: *K1, p1, k1, prb, k1, [yo, k2togtbl] 2 times; rep from *—225 (243, 279, 297, 333) sts.

RND 24: *[P1, k1] 2 times, p1, [k2tog, yo] 2 times; rep from *.

RND 25: *[K1, p1] 2 times, k1, [yo, k2togtbl] 2 times; rep from *.

Rep the last 2 rnds 3 (5, 7, 9, 11) more times, then work Rnd 24 once more.

NEXT RND: *K2, yo, k2togtbl, yo, k1, [yo, k2togtbl] 2 times; rep from *—250 (270, 310, 330, 370) sts.

Change to granite rib patt (see Stitch Guide) and work 3 rnds even, beg and ending with Rnd 1—piece measures about 5¼ (5¾, 6¼, 6¾, 7¼)" (13.5 [14.5, 16, 17, 18.5] cm) from CO.

15½ (16, 16, 16¾, 17¼)"
39.5 (40.5, 40.5, 42.5, 44) cm

5¼ (5¾, 6¼, 6¾, 7¼)"
13.5 (14.5, 16, 17, 18.5) cm

Front & Back

3¾ (4, 4¼, 4½, 5)"
9.5 (10, 11, 11.5, 12.5) cm

12 (13, 14½, 15, 16½)"
30.5 (33, 37, 38, 42) cm

10½"
26.5 cm

33¼ (35½, 40, 42¼, 46¾)"
84.5 (90, 101.5, 107.5, 118.5) cm

37¼ (41¼, 45½, 49½, 53¾)"
94.5 (105, 115.5, 125.5, 136.5) cm

DIVIDE FOR BODY AND SLEEVES

(Rnd 2 of patt) Work 20 (25, 25, 30, 35) sts in established patt for right back, place next 65 (70, 80, 85, 95) sts on holder for right sleeve, use the cable method (see Glossary) to CO 15 sts for right underarm, work 75 (80, 95, 100, 110) sts in patt for front, place next 65 (70, 80, 85, 95) sts on holder for left sleeve, use the cable method to CO 15 sts for left underarm, work 25 (25, 30, 30, 35) sts in patt for left half of back—150 (160, 180, 190, 210) sts total; beg of rnd will not be exactly at center back for all sizes because each section must contain a multiple of 5 sts.

Upper Body

Work in established granite rib patt for 23 (25, 27, 29, 31) more rnds, ending with Rnd 1 of patt—piece measures about 3¾ (4, 4¼, 4½, 5)" (9.5 [10, 11, 11.5, 12.5] cm) from dividing rnd and 9 (9¾, 10½, 11¼, 12¼)" (23 [25, 26.5, 28.5, 31] cm) from CO. NOTE: Try on garment and check to see if it reaches to the underbust. To customize upper body length, work more or fewer reps of patt between dividing rnd and underbust; every 4 rnds added or removed will increase or decrease the upper body length by about ½" (1.3 cm).

NEXT RND: Knit, dec 33 (30, 37, 34, 41) sts evenly spaced, and mark this rnd for underbust—117 (130, 143, 156, 169) sts.

Lower Body

Change to size 4 (3.5 mm) cir needle. Work Rnds 1–8 of 13-st scallop patt (see Stitch Guide) 2 times. Change to size 5 (3.75 mm) cir needle, and work Rnds 1–8 of patt 3 more times—40 patt rnds total; piece measures about 5¼" (13.5 cm) from underbust rnd.

INC RND: (counts as Rnd 1 of 14-st scallop patt) *[Ssk] 2 times, M1 (see Glossary), [k2tog] 2 times, [k1, yo] 4 times, k1; rep from * to end—126 (140, 154, 168, 182) sts.

Work Rnds 2–8 of 14-st scallop patt (see Stitch Guide), then work Rnds 1–8 of patt 2 times.

INC RND: (counts as Rnd 1 of 15-st scallop patt) *[Ssk] 2 times, k1, M1, [k2tog] 2 times, [k1, yo] 4 times, k1; rep from * to end—135 (150, 165, 180, 195) sts.

Work Rnds 2–8 of 15-st scallop patt (see Stitch Guide), then work Rnds 1–8 of patt once more—piece measures about 10½" (26.5 cm) from underbust and 19½ (20¼, 21, 21¾, 22¾)" (49.5 [51.5, 53.5, 55, 58] cm) from CO. NOTE: To customize overall body

length, work more or fewer reps of 15-st scallop patt here; every 4 rnds added or removed will increase or decrease the length by about ½" (1.3 cm). BO all sts pwise.

Sleeve Edging

Place 65 (70, 80, 85, 95) held sleeve sts on size 3 (3.25 mm) dpn. With RS facing, join yarn to center st of 15 CO underarm sts. With dpn, pick up and knit center CO st and place a removable marker or safety pin in this st (not on the needle between sts), pick up and knit 7 more sts from underarm CO, k65 (70, 80, 85, 95) sleeve sts, pick up and knit 7 sts from other side of underarm CO—80 (85, 95, 100, 110) sts total.

RND 1: Purl marked st, p2tog, purl to 2 sts before marked st, p2togtbl (see Glossary)—78 (83, 93, 98, 108) sts.

RND 2: *K1, yo; rep from * to end—156 (166, 186, 196, 216) sts.

RND 3: Purl, dropping each yo as you come to it—78 (83, 93, 98, 108) sts.

RND 4: *K2tog; rep from * to last 0 (1, 1, 0, 0) st, k0 (1, 1, 0, 0)—39 (42, 47, 49, 54) sts; edging measures about 1" (2.5 cm) from pick-up rnd.

With size 4 (3.5 mm) cir needle and using the decrease method (see Glossary), BO all sts loosely. Sleeve opening should measure about 12 (13, 14½, 15, 16½)" (30.5 [33, 37, 38, 42] cm) around; if it is too tight, remove the BO rnd and BO again more loosely or with an even larger needle.

Finishing

Weave in loose ends. Block lightly to measurements, coaxing sleeve sections of yoke upward in a gentle curve to form a scooped neckline as shown on schematic. Beg and end at center back, thread silk fabric strip through neckline eyelet rnd, then tie an overhand knot about 4½" (11.5 cm) from each end of strip. Pull up fabric strip, drawstring-fashion, to where best fit is achieved and tie in a bow at the center back.

enfant SAUVAGE

RUSTIC WITH A GYPSY EDGE

In the heart of every French Girl is a wild child, an *enfant sauvage* who longs to sunbathe *au naturel* or dine on *chèvre* and *vin rouge* curled up on a picnic blanket under the stars. As the daughter of an oyster farmer whose early years were spent on the primordial coast of Washington State, my appreciation of the untamed world is still a deep part of my being. When traveling in France, I continue to be struck by how profoundly rural much of the country is and how venerated the products of field and forest are in the French culture. It is no wonder I feel completely at home there, even among city dwellers, whose daily lives see little separation between farm and table. Burgeoning flower and vegetable markets spring up at every corner.

In Enfant Sauvage, I celebrate the earthy, textural fibers that are still quite close to their source, be it animal or plant. Rustic yet refined, casual yet elegant—the look is approachable and wearable with sculptural stitch elements and cables and tints from the natural dyepot or straight-from-the-sheep colorways. Organic and minimally processed yarns hold sway here, fashioned into garments that draw inspiration from the pearly inner shells of oysters or the swaying stems of bamboo. The smaller companies that produce these heavenly fibers are committed to earth-friendly practices and are finding a wider audience for their offerings. I am heartened to see larger concerns moving in this direction and consider any shift toward sustainability to be most welcome. "Green" is hot and trendy in the marketplace today—I say, it's about time! I invite you to embrace your "nature girl" and discover the pleasure of working with the enticing fibers and designs.

NADINE ✳ *tunic tank*

FINISHED SIZE

33 (36, 38¼, 40¾, 42½)" (84 [91.5, 97, 103.5, 108] cm) bust circumference. Tunic shown measures 36" (91.5 cm).

YARN

Worsted weight (#4 Medium).

SHOWN HERE: Bee Sweet Bambino (70% cotton, 30% bamboo; 100 yd [91 ml/50 g]: #893 spearmint, 7 (8, 8, 9, 9) skeins.

NEEDLES

FRONT AND BACK: size U.S. 7 (4.5 mm): 36" (90 cm) circular (cir). HEM: size U.S. 8 (5 mm) 36" (90 cm) cir. *Adjust needle size if necessary to obtain the correct gauge.*

NOTIONS

Stitch holders; markers (m); removable markers; tapestry needle; smooth cotton waste yarn for provisional cast-on; size H/8 (5 mm) crochet hook.

GAUGE

14 stitches and 22 rows = 4" (10 cm) in reverse stockinette stitch (purl RS rows; knit WS rows) on smaller needle; 19 stitches and 32 rows of lace panel pattern from chart measures 3¾" (9.5 cm) wide and 6¾" (17 cm) high on smaller needle, after blocking.

As a former hippie-chick (actually, not so much former as cleaned up a bit), I support those who make their living with conscience-satisfying undertakings. It makes my heart happy to see the next wave of mostly women-run businesses reaching into communities to help people carve out a decent living for themselves and their children.

Nadine is a *petite homage* to my friend Nadine Curtis, whose company, Bee Sweet, provides just such an avenue for the South African women who produce her juicy, color-saturated yarns. Besides, it's such a cool name for a French Girl. How could I not want to design something called Nadine?

The marriage of soft organic cotton and bamboo twisted together, one taking dye just a smidge differently from the other, makes a garment with dimensional interest. Throw in a leafy Japanese stitch pattern for the lace panels that sidle from front to back, and the result is a nonfussy tunic with femme appeal, very much like Nadine herself.

Notes

- With careful joining and seaming, this garment can be made completely reversible. The body directions are written in reverse stockinette stitch with the purl side of the fabric as the right side, and the charted lace pattern is presented with the predominantly knit side as its right side. The photographs show the garment worn reversed with the knit side of the body and predominantly purl side of the lace panels on the outside to demonstrate that it works equally well.
- The front lace panels are worked separately from the lower edge of the front to the armhole edge, then continue up and over the shoulder line to function as straps. The center front panel is worked from side to side with triangular short-rowed lace inserts at the hem, then grafted between the front lace panels. The sides and back are worked in one piece from side to side with matching lace inserts at the hem and short-row shaping for the hips and bust. The ends of back piece are then grafted to the sides of the front.
- For the lace panels, slip the first stitch of all RS rows as if to purl with yarn in back and slip the first st of all WS rows as if to purl with yarn in front.
- The garter-stitch hem (not shown on schematic) will add about ½" (1.3 cm) to overall length after finishing.

Front

LACE PANELS

With smaller needle and using the cable method (see Glossary), CO 19 sts. Work Rows 1–32 of Lace Panel chart 5 (5, 5, 6, 6) times, then work 8 (16, 24, 0, 8) more rows in patt to end with Row 8 (16, 24, 32, 8) of chart—168 (176, 184, 192, 200) rows completed.

NEXT ROW: (RS) K1, [k2tog] 9 times—10 sts rem.

BO all sts. Make a second panel the same as the first. Pin out each panel to 3¾" (9.5 cm) wide for most of its length, tapering to 2" (5 cm) wide at BO end, and 35½ (37½, 39, 40½, 42½)" (90 [95, 99, 103, 108] cm) long. Mist lightly with water to block, and allow to air-dry thoroughly.

CENTER FRONT PANEL

With smaller needle and using the crochet-on method (see Glossary), provisionally CO 86 sts. Beg with a RS purl row, work even in rev St st (purl RS rows; knit WS rows) for 28 (30, 32, 34, 36) rows, ending with a WS knit row—piece measures about 5 (5½, 5¾, 6¼, 6½)" (12.5 [14, 14.5, 16, 16.5] cm) from CO.

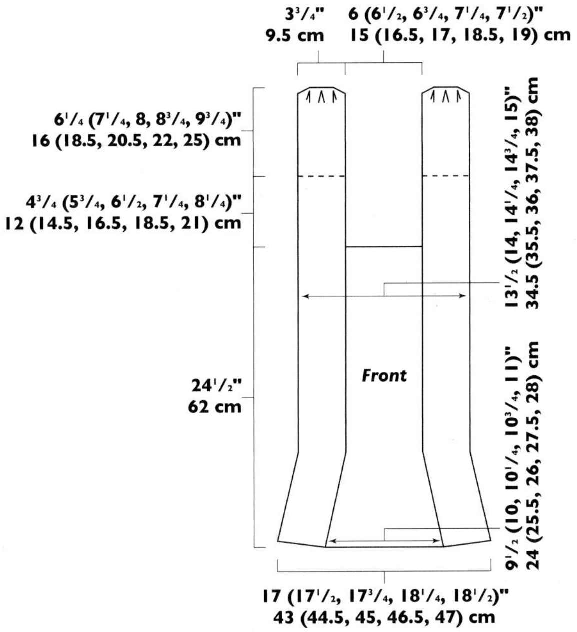
3¾"
9.5 cm
6 (6½, 6¾, 7¼, 7½)"
15 (16.5, 17, 18.5, 19) cm
6¼ (7¼, 8, 8¾, 9¾)"
16 (18.5, 20.5, 22, 25) cm
4¾ (5¾, 6½, 7¼, 8¼)"
12 (14.5, 16.5, 18.5, 21) cm
24½"
62 cm
Front
13½ (14, 14¼, 14¾, 15)"
34.5 (35.5, 36, 37.5, 38) cm
9½ (10, 10¼, 10¾, 11)"
24 (25.5, 26, 27.5, 28) cm
17 (17½, 17¾, 18¼, 18½)"
43 (44.5, 45, 46.5, 47) cm

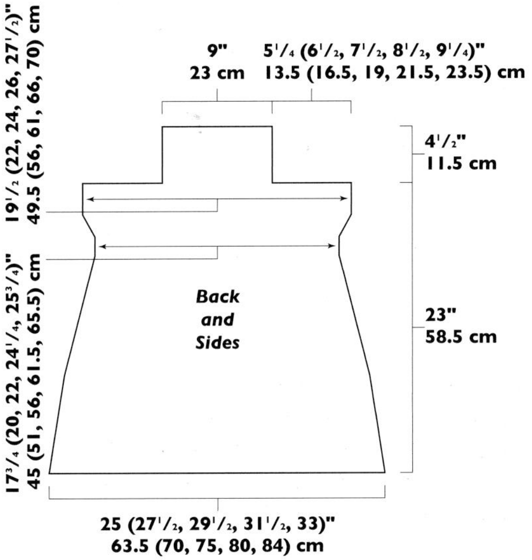
9"
23 cm
5¼ (6½, 7½, 8½, 9¼)"
13.5 (16.5, 19, 21.5, 23.5) cm
19½ (22, 24, 26, 27½)"
49.5 (56, 61, 66, 70) cm
4½"
11.5 cm
17¾ (20, 22, 24¼, 25¾)"
45 (51, 56, 61.5, 65.5) cm
Back
and
Sides
23"
58.5 cm
25 (27½, 29½, 31½, 33)"
63.5 (70, 75, 80, 84) cm

Lace Panel

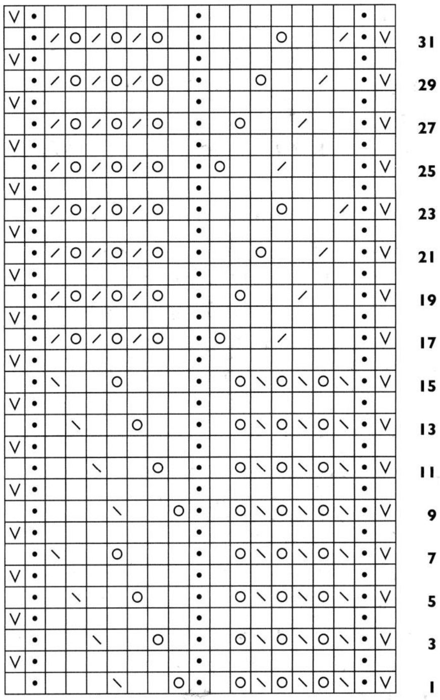
31
29
27
25
23
21
19
17
15
13
11
9
7
5
3
1

- ☐ k on RS; p on WS
- • p on RS; k on WS
- ○ yo
- / k2tog
- \ ssk
- V sl 1 (see Notes)

Left Front Hem Insert

Work short-rows for lace insert at hem edge (beg of RS rows) as foll:

SHORT-ROW 1: (RS) P1, [yo, p2tog] 13 times, turn.

SHORT-ROWS 2, 4, 6, 8, AND 10: Place marker (pm), yo, knit to end.

SHORT-ROW 3: P1, [yo, p2tog] 12 times, turn.

SHORT-ROW 5: P1, [yo, p2tog] 11 times, turn.

SHORT-ROW 7: P1, [yo, p2tog] 10 times, turn.

SHORT-ROW 9: P1, [yo, p2tog] 9 times, turn.

SHORT-ROW 11: *Purl to yo before m, sl yo temporarily to right needle, remove m, return yo to left needle and work yo tog with st after it as p2tog through back loops (tbl); rep from * 4 more times, purl to end—still 86 sts.

Work 2 rows even in rev St st, ending with a RS purl row; piece measures about 7¼ (7¾, 8, 8½, 8¾)" (18.5 [19.5, 20.5, 21.5, 22] cm) from CO at hem edge (beg of RS rows) and 5½ (6, 6¼, 6¾, 7)" (14 [15, 16, 17, 18] cm) from CO at neck edge (end of RS rows). Place sts on holder.

Right Front Hem Insert

Carefully remove waste yarn from provisional CO and place 86 exposed sts on smaller needle. Rejoin yarn with WS (knit side) facing at hem edge. Work short-rows for lace insert at hem edge (beg of WS rows) as foll:

SHORT-ROW 1: (WS) K1, [yo, k2tog] 13 times, turn.

SHORT-ROWS 2, 4, 6, 8, AND 10: (RS) Pm, yo, purl to end.

SHORT-ROW 3: K1, [yo, k2tog] 12 times, turn.

SHORT-ROW 5: K1, [yo, k2tog] 11 times, turn.

SHORT-ROW 7: K1, [yo, k2tog] 10 times, turn.

SHORT-ROW 9: K1, [yo, k2tog] 9 times, turn.

SHORT-ROW 11: *Knit to yo before m, sl yo temporarily to right needle, remove m, return yo to left needle and work yo tog with st after it as k2tog; rep from * 4 more times, knit to end—still 86 sts.

Work 1 RS row even—entire piece measures about 9½ (10, 10¼, 10¾, 11)" (24 [25.5, 26, 27.5, 28] cm) high at hem edge with lace inserts and 6 (6½, 6¾, 7¼, 7½)" (15 [16.5, 17, 18.5, 19] cm) high at neck edge. Place sts on holder.

JOIN CENTER FRONT AND LACE PANELS

With RS of one lace panel facing, measure 24½" (62 cm), or about 116 rows, up from CO edge along selvedge at end of RS rows and place removable marker. With RS facing and smaller needle, join yarn to marked position, then pick up and knit 86 sts along lace panel selvedge from marked position to end (about 3 sts for every 4 rows). With yarn threaded on a tapestry needle, use the Kitchener st (see Glossary) to graft picked-up sts of lace panel to 86 held sts at left end of center front panel (sts worked after left hem insert). With RS of rem lace panel facing, measure 24½" (62 cm), or about 116 rows, up from CO edge along selvedge at beg of RS rows and place removable marker. With RS facing and smaller needle, join yarn to CO edge of lace panel, then pick up and knit 86 sts along lace panel selvedge from CO to marked position (about 3 sts for every 4 rows). With yarn threaded on a tapestry needle, use the Kitchener st to graft picked-up sts of lace panel to 86 held sts at right end of center front panel (sts worked after right hem insert).

Back and Sides

CENTER BACK PANEL

With smaller needle and using the crochet-on method, CO 80 sts. Work 6 (10, 14, 18, 20) rows in rev St st, ending with a WS row.

NEXT ROW: (RS) Purl to end, then use the cable method to CO 15 sts at end of row for upper back extension—95 sts.

Work even in rev St st until piece measures 9" (23 cm) from sts CO at start of upper back extension, ending with a RS row.

NEXT ROW: (WS) BO 15 upper back sts, knit to end—80 sts rem.

Work even in rev St st for 6 (10, 14, 18, 20) rows, ending with a WS row—piece measures about 11½ (13, 14½, 16, 16½)" (29 [33, 37, 40.5, 42] cm) high at hem edge (beg of RS rows).

RIGHT HIP SHAPING

Work short-rows for hip shaping as foll:

SHORT-ROW 1: (RS) P60, turn.

SHORT-ROWS 2, 4, 6, 8, AND 10: (WS) Pm, yo, knit to end.

SHORT-ROW 3: P58, turn.

SHORT-ROW 5: P56, turn.

SHORT-ROW 7: P54, turn.

SHORT-ROW 9: P52, turn.

SHORT-ROW 11: *Purl to yo before m, sl yo temporarily to right needle, remove m, return yo to left needle and work yo tog with st after it as p2togtbl (see Glossary); rep from * 4 more times, purl to end—still 80 sts. Knit 1 WS row.

RIGHT BACK HEM INSERT

Work Short-rows 1–11 as for left front hem insert, beg ending with a RS row. Work even in rev St st for 7 (11, 11, 13, 15) rows, beg ending with a WS row. Purl 1 RS row—piece measures about 17¼ (19¼, 21, 22¾, 23¾)" (44 [49, 53.5, 58, 60.5] cm) high at hem edge.

RIGHT BUST SHAPING

Work short-rows for bust shaping at armhole edge (beg of WS rows) as foll:

SHORT-ROW 1: (WS) K15, turn.

SHORT-ROWS 2, 4, AND 6: (RS) Pm, yo, knit to end.

SHORT-ROW 3: K12, turn.

SHORT-ROW 5: K9, turn.

SHORT-ROW 7: *Knit to yo before m, sl yo temporarily to right needle, remove m, return yo to left needle and work yo tog with st after it as k2tog; rep from * 2 more times, knit to end—still 80 sts.

Work even in rev St st for 4 rows, ending with a WS row—piece measures about 18¼ (20¼, 22, 23¾, 24¾)" (46.5 [51.5, 56, 60.5, 63] cm) high at hem edge and about 5¼ (6½, 7½, 8½, 9¼)" (13.5 [16.5, 19, 21.5, 23.5] cm) from where 15 upper back sts were BO at armhole edge. Place sts on holder.

LEFT HIP SHAPING

Carefully remove waste yarn from provisional CO and place 80 exposed sts on smaller needle. Rejoin yarn with WS facing at

hem edge. Work short-rows for hip shaping as foll:

SHORT-ROW 1: (WS) K60, turn.

SHORT-ROWS 2, 4, 6, 8, AND 10: (RS) Pm, yo, purl to end.

SHORT-ROW 3: K58, turn.

SHORT-ROW 5: K56, turn.

SHORT-ROW 7: K54, turn.

SHORT-ROW 9: K52, turn.

SHORT-ROW 11: *Knit to yo before m, sl yo temporarily to right needle, remove m, return yo to left needle and work yo tog with st after it as k2tog; rep from * 4 more times, knit to end—still 80 sts.

Purl 1 RS row.

LEFT BACK HEM INSERT

Work Short-rows 1–11 as for right front hem insert, ending with a WS row—80 sts. Work even in rev St st for 8 (12, 12, 14, 16) rows, ending with a WS row—piece measures about 24 (26½, 28½, 30½, 32)" (61 [67.5, 72.5, 77.5, 81.5] cm) high at hem edge.

LEFT BUST SHAPING

Work short-rows for bust shaping at armhole edge (beg of RS rows) as foll:

SHORT-ROW 1: (RS) P15, turn.

SHORT-ROWS 2, 4, AND 6: (RS) Pm, yo, purl to end.

SHORT-ROW 3: P12, turn.

SHORT-ROW 5: P9, turn.

SHORT-ROW 7: *Purl to yo before m, sl yo temporarily to right needle, remove m, return yo to left needle and work yo tog with st after it as p2togtbl; rep from * 2 more times, purl to end—still 80 sts.

Work even in rev St st for 5 rows, beg and ending with a WS row—piece measures about 25 (27½, 29½, 31½, 33)" (63.5 [70, 75, 80, 84] cm) high at hem edge and about 5¼ (6½, 7½, 8½, 9¼)" (13.5 [16.5, 19, 21.5, 23.5] cm) from where 15 upper back sts were CO at armhole edge. Place sts on holder.

Join Front to Back and Sides

Block pieces to measurements. With RS of front facing, measure 23" (58.5 cm), or about 108 rows, up from CO edge along selvedge at beg left lace panel and place removable marker. With RS facing and smaller needle, join yarn to CO edge of front, then pick up and knit 80 sts along lace panel selvedge from CO edge to marked position (about 3 sts for every 4 rows). With yarn threaded on a tapestry needle, use the Kitchener st to graft picked-up sts of lace panel to 80 held sts at left end of back (sts worked after left bust shaping). With RS of front facing, measure 23" (58.5 cm), or about 108 rows, up from CO edge along selvedge at end of right lace panel and place removable marker. With RS facing and smaller needle, join yarn to marked position, then pick up and knit 80 sts along lace panel selvedge from marked position to CO edge (about 3 sts for every 4 rows). With yarn threaded on a tapestry needle, use the Kitchener st to graft picked-up sts of lace panel to 80 held sts at right end of back (sts worked after right bust shaping).

Finishing

STRAPS

Lay garment flat with RS of back facing up. Fold the top 6¼ (7¼, 8, 8¾, 9¾)" (16 [18.5, 20.5, 22, 25] cm) of each lace panel to the back along the shoulder line (dotted line on schematic) so the tapered BO end meets the underarm selvedge. With yarn threaded on tapestry needle, sew BO ends of straps selvedge of back, leaving about a 3¼ (4½, 5½, 6½, 7¼)" (8.5 [11.5, 14, 16.5, 18.5] cm) space between the straps at each underarm. With yarn threaded on a tapestry needle, sew neck selvedge of each strap to BO or CO edge on each side of upper back extension. With crochet hook and RS facing, join yarn to beg of gap between straps at underarm. Work 1 row of single crochet (sc; see Glossary) across underarm selvedge, then along armhole edge of strap, and join with a sl st in first sc. Fasten off last st. Work 1 row of sc around other armhole opening in the same manner.

HEM

With RS facing, smaller needle, and beg at grafted join between left front lace panel and back, pick up and knit 168 (184, 190, 200, 206) sts evenly around lower edge of garment (about 4 sts for each 1" [2.5 cm]). Pm and join for working in rnds. Change to larger needle. Purl 1 rnd, then BO all sts as if to purl on next rnd.

Weave in loose ends. Block again if desired.

NADINE

WRENNA * *leather-laced cardigan*

The Pacific Northwest is a haven for writers and artists, who *sprout up overnight like fairy mushrooms after a good rain.* Perhaps it's the two-thirds of the year we look out on a gray horizon that encourages so much inner expression. I like to think it's our wildly pioneer spirit instead.

Jitterbug Perfume, written by Washington State literary legend Tom Robbins, combines some of my most beloved elements in a book: history, fantasy, and, of course, perfume. In the novel, the character Wrenna inhabited an anonymous circa Dark Ages Eastern European country. A clever girl, she definitely deserved a larger wardrobe than her daily furs and homespun linens afforded.

The Wrenna design, worked in luscious, roving-like, Twinkle Soft Chunky yarn, looks as if it could have sprung from our Seattle skies. Top-down construction and leather lacings make for ease of construction and malleable fit. Arrowhead motifs worked at an oversize gauge take on a primitive quality, reminding me of eleventh-century stone carvings in the rustic country chapels of France—the pagan and the Christian entwined. Perhaps Mr. Robbins would approve.

FINISHED SIZE

37½ (39¾, 42, 44)" (95 [101, 106.5, 112] cm) bust circumference. Sweater shown measures 37½" (95 cm).

YARN

Chunky weight (#5 Bulky).

SHOWN HERE: Twinkle Soft Chunky (100% wool; 83 yd [76 ml/200 g): #51 hazel, 3 (4, 4, 5) skeins.

NEEDLES

YOKE AND LOWER BODY: size U.S. 17 (12.75 mm): 36" (90 cm) circular (cir). SLEEVE EDGING: size U.S. 15 (10 mm) 12" (30 cm) cir; double-pointed needles (dpn) may be substituted for shorter cir. *Adjust needle size if necessary to obtain the correct gauge.*

NOTIONS

Markers (m); tapestry needle; size N/15 (10 mm) crochet hook; 54" (138 cm) leather or ultra suede lacing ¼" (6 mm) wide (available from fabric or craft stores).

GAUGE

13 stitches = 7" (18 cm) wide and 13 rows = 5" (12.5 cm) high in stockinette stitch on larger needles; 15 stitches and 13 rows in horseshoe lace pattern from chart = 7" (18 cm) wide and 5" (12.5 cm) high on larger needles.

Notes

- The yoke is worked in one piece from the neck edge down to the underarms where stitches are put on holders for the armhole openings. The front and back are worked in one piece to the lower edge, then the sleeve edgings are worked in the round from the underarms.
- Slip the first st of all RS rows as if to purl with yarn in back; slip the first st of all WS rows as if to purl with yarn in front.

Stitch Guide

TWISTED DOUBLE DECREASE
Sl 2 sts as if to k2tog through their back loops, k1, pass 2 slipped sts over—2 sts dec'd.

Yoke

With size 17 (12.75 mm) cir needle and using the cable method (see Glossary), CO 61 sts for all sizes.

ROW 1: (RS) Sl 1 (see Notes), *k1, p1; rep from *.

ROW 2: Sl 1, *p1, k1; rep from *.

ROWS 3–6: Rep Rows 1 and 2 two times—piece measures about 2¼″ (5.5 cm) from CO.

ROW 7: Sl 1, k5, M1 (see Glossary), [k7, M1] 7 times, k6—69 sts.

ROWS 8 AND 10: Sl 1, purl to end.

ROW 9: Sl 1, k2, M1, [k8, M1] 8 times, k2—78 sts.

ROW 11: Sl 1, k8, M1, [k12, M1] 5 times, k9—84 sts.

ROW 12: Sl 1, p17 for right front, place marker (pm) for right front raglan, p9 for right sleeve, pm for right back raglan, p30 for back, pm for left back raglan, p9 for left sleeve, pm for left front raglan, p18 for left front.

ROW 13: Sl 1, k1, work Row 1 of Horseshoe Lace chart over next 15 sts (work red patt rep box only once), k1f&b (see Glossary) in last st of left front, sl m, *k1f&b, knit to 1 st before next m, k1f&b, sl m; rep from * 2 more times, k1&b, work Row 1 of Horseshoe Lace chart over next 15 sts (work red patt rep box only once), k2—92 sts; 19 sts each front, 32 back sts, 11 sts each sleeve.

ROW 14: Sl 1, work in patt to end, working sts outside chart sections in St st.

ROW 15: Sl 1, work in established patts to last left front st, k1f&b, sl m, *k1f&b, knit to 1 st before next m, k1f&b, sl m; rep from * 2 more times, k1&b, work in established patts to end—100 sts; 20 sts each front; 34 back sts; 13 sts each sleeve.

ROW 16: Rep Row 14.

Rep the last 2 rows 0 (1, 1, 2) more time(s)—100 (108, 108, 116) sts; 20 (21, 21, 22) sts each front; 34 (36, 36, 38) back sts; 13 (15, 15, 17) sts each sleeve.

SLEEVE INC ROW: (RS) Sl 1, work in patts to end of left front, *sl m, k1f&b, knit to 1 st before next m, k1f&b, sl m,* knit across back sts; rep from * to * for second sleeve, work in patts to end of right front—4 sts inc'd, 2 sts each sleeve.

Horseshoe Lace

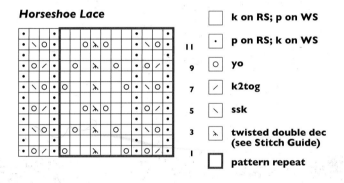

☐	k on RS; p on WS
·	p on RS; k on WS
O	yo
╱	k2tog
╲	ssk
⅄	twisted double dec (see Stitch Guide)
☐	pattern repeat

Work 1 WS row even [Work sleeve inc row, work 1 WS row even] 2 (3, 4, 4) more times, ending with Row 10 (2, 4, 6) of chart—112 (124, 128, 136) sts; 20 (21, 21, 22) sts each front; 34 (36, 36, 38) back sts; 19 (23, 25, 27) sts each sleeve; piece measures about 8½ (10, 10¾, 11½)" (21.5 [25.5, 27.5, 29] cm) from CO.

DIVIDE FOR BODY AND SLEEVES

(RS) Removing m as you come to them, work 19 (20, 20, 21) sts as established for left front, place next 21 (25, 27, 29) sts on holder for left sleeve, use the cable method to CO 2 (2, 4, 4) for left underarm, k32 (34, 34, 36) back sts, place next 21 (25, 27, 29) sts on holder for right sleeve, CO 2 (2, 4, 4) sts for right underarm, work 19 (20, 20, 21) sts as established for right front—74 (78, 82, 86) sts.

Lower Body

Cont established patts on fronts and working rem sts in St st, work 6 (2, 6, 4) rows even, ending with Row 5 (5, 11, 11) of chart.

NEXT ROW: (WS) Work 17 sts in patt, dec 1 (dec 1, inc 2, inc 2) st(s) evenly spaced over center 40 (44, 48, 52) sts, work last 17 sts in patt—73 (77, 84, 88) sts.

NEXT ROW: (RS) Work 17 sts in established patts, work 1 (3, 1, 3) St st(s), work Row 7 (7, 1, 1) of Horseshoe Lace chart over center 37 (37, 48, 48) sts, work 1 (3, 1, 3) st(s) in St st, work 17 sts in established patts.

Cont to sl first st of every row and work sts outside charted sections in St st, work 5 rows even in patts, ending with Row 12 (12, 6, 6) of chart.

SIDE INC ROW: (RS) Work 17 sts in patt, M1, work in patt to last 17 sts, M1, work in patt to end—2 sts inc'd.

Working new sts in St st, work 5 rows even in patt, then rep the side inc row on next RS row—77 (81, 88, 92) sts; 3 (5, 3, 5) sts in St st between horseshoe lace patts at each side.

NEXT ROW: (WS) Work 17 sts in patt, [p1, k1] 1 (2, 1, 2) time(s), p1, work established patt over center 37 (37, 48, 48) sts, [p1, k1] 1 (2, 1, 2) time(s), p1, work in patt to end.

Working sts between charted sections as they appear (knit the knits and purl the purls), work even for 4 (10, 4, 10) more rows, ending with Row 12 (6, 6, 12) of chart—piece measures about 9½ (10¼, 9½, 11¼)" (24 [26, 24, 28.5] cm) from where body and sleeves divided.

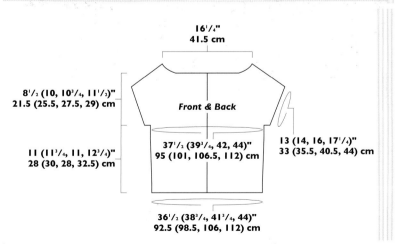

16¼"
41.5 cm

Front & Back

8½ (10, 10¾, 11½)"
21.5 (25.5, 27.5, 29) cm

11 (11¾, 11, 12¾)"
28 (30, 28, 32.5) cm

37½ (39¾, 42, 44)"
95 (101, 106.5, 112) cm

13 (14, 16, 17¼)"
33 (35.5, 40.5, 44) cm

36½ (38¾, 41¾, 44)"
92.5 (98.5, 106, 112) cm

NEXT ROW: (RS) *K1, p1; rep from * to last st and *at the same time* dec 0 (0, 1, 1) st near center back, end k1—77 (81, 87, 91) sts.

Work all sts in rib as they appear for 3 more rows, ending with a WS row—piece measures about 11 (11³/₄, 11, 12³/₄)" (28 [30, 28, 32.5] cm) from dividing row and about 19¹/₂ (21³/₄, 21³/₄, 24¹/₄)" (49.5 [55, 55, 61.5] cm) from CO at neck edge. BO all sts loosely in rib patt.

Sleeve Edgings

Place 21 (25, 27, 29) held sleeve sts on smaller cir needle or dpn. Join yarn with RS facing beg of sts CO at underarm.

NEXT RND: Pick up and knit 3 (1, 3, 3) st(s) from CO sts, k21 (25, 27, 29) sleeve sts, pm, and join for working in rnds—24 (26, 30, 32) sts.

NEXT RND: *K1, p1; rep from * to end.

BO all sts in rib patt.

Finishing

Weave in loose ends. Block to measurements, coaxing sleeve sections of yoke upward in a gentle curve to form a scooped neckline as shown on schematic.

FRONT EDGING

With RS facing, join yarn to lower right front corner. With crochet hook (see Glossary for crochet instructions) *ch2, work crochet sl st in next slipped selvedge st of body; rep from * to end, then fasten off last st. With RS facing, join yarn to upper left front corner, and work crochet edging in the same manner.

LACING

Beg at base of neck ribbing, lace front edges tog for 5" (12.5 cm) or for desired length, by threading leather cord back and forth, shoelace-fashion, through ch-2 spaces along front edges as shown. Draw up cord until front edges meet and tie at bottom of lacing as shown.

Having a perfectly fitting knitted garment begins and ends in the same place—with you. Though it might seem obvious to say, your own body is where your shaping must originate and where adjustments will need to be made. I encourage you to make a study of it. We designers—and the technical editors who support us so brilliantly—endeavor to provide the best calculations possible for garment instructions. But because our bodies are more variable than any set of numbers, a bit of customizing is often necessary to get a perfect fit. Customization is especially important for seamless knitting. Finessing complex patterns into a one-piece mode can be challenging, and the price of no-sew construction is the need to participate in the process.

Let us begin then at the atomic level, so to speak—your chosen yarn and the gauge swatch. For me, the swatch holds more weight than any measurement. The excellent tutorial on swatching in *No Sheep for You* by Amy R. Singer will give you a thorough understanding of what happens to knitted fabric in the real world. You can't rely on the adorable little unwashed, unblocked 4″ (10 cm) square you may think will tell you how your knitted fabric will behave.

After you've knitted, washed, and blocked your swatch, you can be more confident about the properties of your yarn. Now, you can make decisions about sizing (e.g., the length of the sleeves or bodice) as you knit. You will know rather than guess what will happen with the finished garment. I encourage you to keep your swatches and notes about your projects in a notebook, so you can refer back to them whenever you want.

Stopping to try on a garment multiple times in the course of knitting isn't the most relaxing way to knit, and I understand the lure of curling up and knitting for hours of mindless pleasure. But for this book's projects, let's focus on how to create your personal knitting roadmap for mindful knitting.

I believe in simplicity (all those volumes of Zen Buddhist poetry I read in the 1970s left their mark). To that end, I urge you to streamline your knitting life:

- Take time to discover which styles of knitted garments look best on your body. A trip to a variety of shops with a friend and a full-length mirror at the ready can open your eyes to new possibilities and, thankfully, slam the door shut on others before you cast on a single stitch.

- Network with those who have knitted the object of your affection. Doing so has now been made ever so much easier because of the phenomenal resource of Ravelry (ravelry.com), which lets you see how a garment looks on real knitters in multiple sizes and colors. Knitting circles and guilds also give you opportunities to share triumphs and failures and to be inspired and educated by what others have made.

- Avail yourself of online resources that generously offer loads of information at no charge. Two of my favorites are *Knitty* (knitty.com), whose informational articles are a massive knitting book in themselves, not to mention the wonderful patterns, and Interweave's *Knitting Daily* (knittingdaily.com), which has excellent tutorials on measuring yourself and recipes for shaping, as well as a genius photo gallery of the same garment on women of many sizes.

- Develop an understanding of your knitting preferences—a more fitted armhole, for example, or a waist that might require more shaping than a pattern calls for. Know these idiosyncrasies before you begin a garment.

- Have a friend help you take your own measurements. Also, consider purchasing a dress form.

For additional information, please refer to the excellent in-depth articles and tutorials listed in the Bibliography. The more you educate yourself and pay attention to what works best for you, the more confident you'll become.

TOP-DOWN SEAMLESS RAGLAN CONSTRUCTION

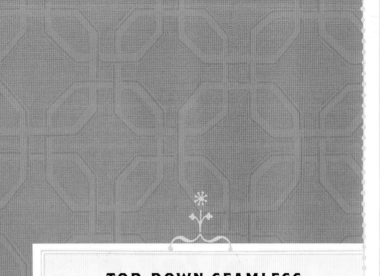

The beauty of top-down raglans is their simplicity and ease of construction. You can achieve a perfect fit by trying on the garment as you go and making custom adjustments along the way.

A top-down raglan begins with the number of stitches required for the neck circumference. The four body sections (front, back, right sleeve, and left sleeve) are delineated by markers, which indicate where increases will be made to shape the yoke (Figure 1). The increases create diagonal lines that follow the boundaries between the four body sections as you work the distance from the neck to the armhole. In *Knitting from the Top,* Barbara Walker visually documents an impressive variety of

possible increases. You'll need longer needles as the number of stitches increases.

At the armholes, you place the sleeve stitches on holders to be worked later and add a few extra underarm stitches across the gaps. You rejoin the front and back and work them as a unit to the hem, adding bust, waist, and hip shaping along the way (Figure 2). You then place the held sleeve stitches on needles (on either one short circular needle or three or four double-pointed needles), add a few extra stitches at the underarm, and work the stitches in rounds to the cuff (Figure 3). The sweaters that use this type of construction are Simone (page 100) and Martine (page 120). Paloma (page 32) and Wrenna (page 48) are worked in modifications of this technique.

For a pullover, you work the yoke and body in rounds. Simply cast on the desired number of stitches for the back, then the right sleeve, the front, and finally the left sleeve, placing a marker between each section. Join for working in rounds. Unless otherwise specified, the round begins at the left back neck. For a cardigan, you work the stitches back and forth in rows, beginning and ending at the center front. Cast on stitches first for the left front, then the left sleeve, the back, the right sleeve, and finally the right front, placing a marker between each section. For a pullover with a placket neckline, begin as for a cardigan, working back and forth in rows for the depth of the placket, then join the stitches for working in rounds to the hem.

Many of the projects in this book involve waist shaping. In most cases, paired decreases—decreases that lean to the right paired with decreases that lean to the left—are used to narrow the body at the waist, then "invisible" increases are worked to widen the body to accommodate the hips. Before you bind off at the hem, try on the garment and make sure that you're comfortable with the final length. It's a small matter to add or remove a few rows of knitting to get the length you want.

FIGURE 1

FIGURE 2

FIGURE 3

TIPS FOR TOP-DOWN RAGLAN CONSTRUCTION

- An important consideration in constructing a top-down raglan garment is the shoulder width. For example, if you have narrow shoulders and a large bust, consider following the instructions for a size smaller than usual to get the proper fit for the upper yoke, then add the necessary room at the underarm by casting on more stitches at the body join and/or working short-rows in the bust area.

- The increases worked along raglan seam lines can accentuate the shoulders and bust, which isn't always advantageous. Especially in silhouettes that feature a crew or high neckline, I often design raglans to have a more open (broad and/or deep) or V-neck shape to help minimize the emphasis on shoulders and bust and highlight instead women's lovely necks and cleavage.

- Sometimes, the number of increases necessary to make the yoke fit between the neck and armhole can inadvertently make the sleeves too wide, especially for those whose upper arms are thin. If this occurs, you can alter the increases, working more on the body (i.e., the front and back) than on the sleeve sides of the raglan seam lines. You'll want to try on the garment often to check your progress.

- Pay special attention to the underarm area because it's easy for the sleeve and body width to grow rapidly as the raglan increases are made in this area, resulting in excess fabric and a baggy look. To control the excess, add extra stitches or short-rows only where needed at the bodice join and/or bust.

STELLA ✳ *cable and lace jacket*

Which comes first, the yarn that inspires the design or the design that calls for the yarn? I never know which will strike that initial spark. Stella's cosmic genesis was in that most basic of places, a humble stitch pattern. I was intrigued by what would happen if I experimented with its swirling motif (usually worked in the round) and morphed it into a flat incarnation. Ah, surprise—biasing panels. Then the fun began. I found a basic yet drapey Aran-weight yarn and paired it with the tiniest strand of sparkling mohair/silk. Perfection! And Stella ("star," in Italian) was born.

If you begin with the sleeves, worked from bottom to top, it's easy to get a handle on the mechanics of the four-round repeat. You then go on to those intriguing biasing side/back panels with some seed-stitch short-rows to complete the front. The sleeves and lower bodice are joined up, stitches manipulated and decreased, and before you know it, you're racing toward the oversize mandarin collar finish line. And surprise again—no seams to sew!

FINISHED SIZE

33 (38½, 44, 49½)" (84 [98, 112, 125.5] cm) bust circumference, with fronts meeting at center. Sweater shown measures 38½" (98 cm).

YARN

Worsted weight (#4 Medium) and sport-weight (#2 Fine).

SHOWN HERE: RYC Cashsoft Aran (57% merino, 33% microfiber, 10% cashmere; 95 yd [87 ml/50 g]): #13 cream, 12 (13, 16, 18) balls.

Rowan Kidsilk Night (67% kid mohair, 18% silk, 10% polyester, 5% nylon; 227 yd [208 ml/25 g]): #607 starlight, 5 (6, 7, 8) balls. NOTE: This yarn has been discontinued; substitute Rowan Kidsilk Haze or the laceweight mohair/silk yarn of your choice.

NEEDLES

SLEEVES: sizes U.S. 9 and 10 (5.5 and 6 mm): 16" (40 cm) circular (cir) or set of 4 or 5 double-pointed (dpn). LOWER BODY: size U.S. 9 (5.5 mm): 36" (90 cm) cir. YOKE: size U.S. 8 (5 mm): 36" (90 cm) cir. COLLAR AND FRONT BIND-OFF: size U.S. 7 (4.5 cm): 24" and 36" (60 and 90 cm) cir. *Adjust needle size if necessary to obtain the correct gauge.*

NOTIONS

Markers (m); removable markers; stitch holders; size H/8 (5 mm) crochet hook; tapestry needle.

GAUGE

All gauges are with one strand of each yarn held together (see Notes). 15½ stitches and 19½ rounds = 4" (10 cm) in 12-stitch spiral-stitch patterns at lower edges of sleeves on size 10 (6 mm) needle; 17½ stitches and 20 rounds = 4" (10 cm) in 10-stitch spiral-stitch patterns in upper sleeves on size 9 (5.5 mm) needle; 16 stitches and 20 rows = 4" (10 cm) in pattern from lower body chart on size 9 (5.5 mm) needle; 12 stitches and 25 rows = 4" (10 cm) in seed stitch on size 9 (5.5 mm) needle; 14 stitches and 26 rows = 4" (10 cm) in seed stitch on size 8 (5 mm) needle.

Notes

The spiral patterns naturally bias to create the swirled effect shown. The bias creates the appearance of faux V-neck shaping because the two sides of the neck opening lean away from each other. It also causes the lower corners of the front to hang about 3" (7.5 cm) lower than center back when blocked.

The decreases of the main two spiral patterns are deliberately not mirror images of each other, even though the patterns themselves bias in opposite directions. The decreases that are part of the main pattern repeats are either k2tog or p2tog, which both slant to the right on the RS.

Do not measure the gauge of the biased spiral patterns following a single tilted column of stitches or a single slanted row. Measure stitch gauge with the ruler held horizontally and parallel to the cast-on edge and measure row gauge with the ruler held vertically and perpendicular to the cast-on edge. The stitches and rows of the bias fabric will lie at an angle to the ruler when measuring in each direction.

The sleeves and lower body are worked separately to the underarms, then joined for working the yoke and collar in one piece. The back yoke is raised slightly with short-rows in the seed-stitch section so the front neck edges are lower than the back neck.

Measurements shown on the schematic include the width of the 1¾" (4.5 cm) seed-stitch front edgings at the bustline, but these bands add only ½" (1.3 cm) to the width of each front at the lower edge because the bands are tapered with short-rows.

For the slipped stitches shown on the charts, slip the first stitch on RS rows as if to purl with yarn in back, and slip the first stitch on WS rows as if to purl with yarn in front.

Stitch Guide

PRB

Purl into st in the row below the next st on left needle—1 st inc'd.

TWISTED DOUBLE DECREASE

Sl 2 sts as if to k2tog through their back loops, k1, pass 2 slipped sts over the knitted st (p2sso)—2 sts dec'd.

SEED STITCH

ROW 1: *K1, p1; rep from *, ending k1 if there is an odd number of sts.

ROW 2: Purl the knits and knit the purls as they appear.

Repeat Row 2 for pattern.

Sleeves

You may find it helpful to mark each sleeve as right or left as it is completed.

RIGHT SLEEVE

With size 10 (6 mm) 16" (40 cm) cir needle or dpn and using the cable method (see Glossary), CO 60 (60, 72, 84) sts. Do not join. To avoid twisting the sts, work Rnd 1 as a RS row to last st, place marker (pm) on needle, then join for working in rnds.

RND 1: *K3, k2tog, k4, yo, p3; rep from *.

RND 2: *K2, k2tog, k4, yo, k1, p3; rep from *.

RND 3: *K1, k2tog, k4, yo, k2, p3; rep from *.

RND 4: *K2tog, k4, yo, k3, p3; rep from *.

RNDS 5–32: Rep Rnds 1–4 seven more times—32 rnds completed; piece measures about 6½" (16.5 cm) from CO (see Notes).

RND 33: *K3, k2tog, k4, yo, p3tog through back loops (tbl); rep from *—50 (50, 60, 70) sts rem.

RND 34: *K2, k2tog, k4, yo, k1, p1; rep from *.

RND 35: *K1, k2tog, k4, yo, k2, p1; rep from *.

RND 36: *K2tog, k4, yo, k3, p1; rep from *.

RND 37: *K3, k2tog, k4, yo, p1: rep from *.

RND 38: Rep Rnd 34.

RND 39: Rep Rnd 35.

RND 40: Rep Rnd 36.

RNDS 41–48: Rep Rnds 37–40 two more times—piece measures about 9¾" (25 cm) from CO.

RNDS 49–108: Change to size 9 (5.5 mm) cir needle or dpn. Rep Rnds 37–40 fifteen more times—piece measures about 21¾" (55 cm) from CO.

To customize sleeve length, work more or fewer reps of Rnds 37–40; every 4 rnds added or removed will lengthen or shorten the sleeve by about ¾" (2 cm). Place first 10 (10, 12, 14) sts on holder for underarm, then place rem 40 (40, 48, 56) sts on separate holder.

LEFT SLEEVE

With size 10 (6 mm) 16" (40 cm) cir needle or dpn and using the cable method, CO 60 (60, 72, 84) sts. Do not join. To avoid twisting, work Rnd 1 as a RS row to last st, place marker (pm) on needle, then join for working in rnds.

RND 1: *P3, yo, k4, k2tog, k3; rep from *.

RND 2: *P3, k1, yo, k4, k2tog, k2; rep from *.

RND 3: *P3, k2, yo, k4, k2tog, k1; rep from *.

RND 4: *P3, k3, yo, k4, k2tog; rep from *.

RNDS 5–32: Rep Rnds 1–4 seven more times—32 rnds completed; piece measures about 6½" (16.5 cm) from CO.

RND 33: *P3tog through back loops, yo, k4, k2tog, k3; rep from *—50 (50, 60, 70) sts rem.

RND 34: *P1, k1, yo, k4, k2tog, k2; rep from *.

RND 35: *P1, k2, yo, k4, k2tog, k1; rep from *.

RND 36: *P1, k3, yo, k4, k2tog; rep from *.

RND 37: *P1, yo, k4, k2tog, k3; rep from *.

RND 38: Rep Rnd 34.

RND 39: Rep Rnd 35.

RND 40: Rep Rnd 36.

RNDS 41–48: Rep Rnds 37–40 two more times—piece measures about 9¾" (25 cm) from CO.

RNDS 49–108: Change to size 9 (5.5 mm) cir needle or dpn. Rep Rnds 37–40 fifteen more times, or for same number of reps as right sleeve—piece measures about 21¾" (55 cm) from CO or

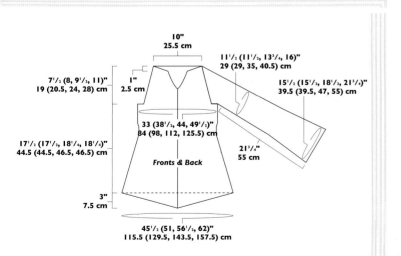

10"
25.5 cm

11½ (11½, 13¾, 16)"
29 (29, 35, 40.5) cm

7½ (8, 9½, 11)"
19 (20.5, 24, 28) cm

1"
2.5 cm

15½ (15½, 18½, 21¾)"
39.5 (39.5, 47, 55) cm

33 (38½, 44, 49½)"
84 (98, 112, 125.5) cm

17½ (17½, 18¼, 18¼)"
44.5 (44.5, 46.5, 46.5) cm

Fronts & Back

21¾"
55 cm

3"
7.5 cm

45½ (51, 56½, 62)"
115.5 (129.5, 143.5, 157.5) cm

Lower Body

57
55
53
51
49
47
45
43
41
39
37
35
33
31
29
27
25
23
21
19
17
15
13
11
9
7
5
3
1
P
P
work 5 (6, 7, 8) times
work 5 (6, 7, 8) times

Yoke

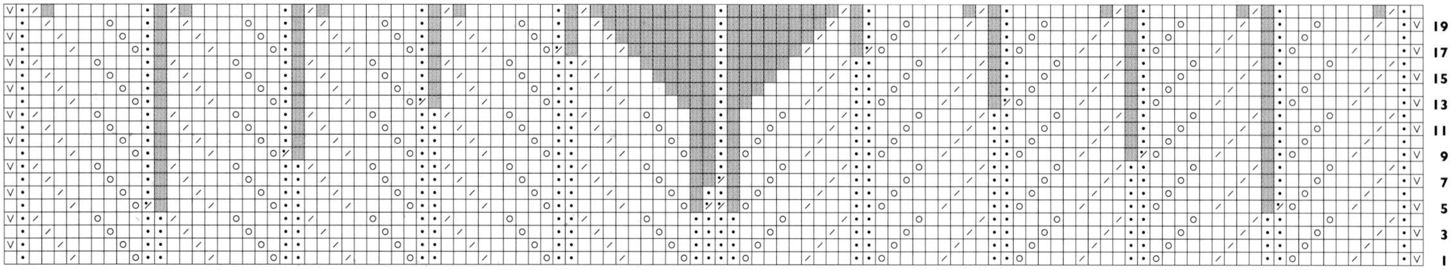
19
17
15
13
11
9
7
5
3
1

Right Front

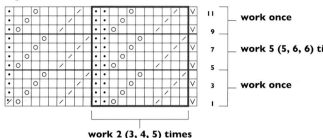

— work once ⎯ 11

— work once ⎯ 9

— work 5 (5, 6, 6) times ⎯ 7

— work once ⎯ 5

— work once ⎯ 3

⎯ 1

work 2 (3, 4, 5) times

Left Front

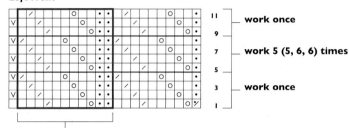

— work once ⎯ 11

— work once ⎯ 9

— work 5 (5, 6, 6) times ⎯ 7

⎯ 5

— work once ⎯ 3

⎯ 1

work 2 (3, 4, 5) times

▢	**k on RS; p on WS**
▫	**p on RS; k on WS**
○	**yo**
╱	**k2tog on RS; p2tog on WS**
↘	**p2tog on RS**
⋏	**twisted double dec (see Stitch Guide)**
P	**prb (see Stitch Guide)**
V	**sl 1 (see Notes)**
▦	**no stitch**
▢	**pattern repeat**

desired length. Place first 10 (10, 12, 14) sts on holder for under-arm, then place rem 40 (40, 48, 56) sts on separate holder.

Lower Body

With size 9 (5.5 mm) 36″ (40 cm) cir needle and using the cable method, CO 178 (200, 222, 244) sts. Do not join. Working back and forth in rows, work Rows 1–58 of Lower Body chart—129 (151, 173, 195) sts; piece measures about 11½″ (29 cm) from CO.

NEXT ROW: (RS) Sl 1, [k1, k2tog, k4, yo, k2, p2] 3 (4, 5, 6) times, [k1, k2tog, k4, yo, k2, p2tog] 2 times, k1, p1, k1, k2tog, k2, p3tog (center sts), k2, k2tog, k1, p1, k1, [p2tog, k2, yo, k4, k2tog, k1] 2 times, [p2, k2, yo, k4, k2tog, k1] 3 (4, 5, 6) times, k1—121 (143, 165, 187) sts.

NEXT ROW: (WS) Sl 1, [p2tog, p4, yo, p3, k2] 3 (4, 5, 6) times, [p2tog, p2, p2tog, yo, p3, k1] 2 times, p1, k1, [p2tog] 2 times, p1, [p2tog] 2 times, k1, p1, [k1, p3, yo, p2tog, p2, p2tog] 2 times, [k2, p3, yo, p4, p2tog] 3 (4, 5, 6) times, p1—113 (135, 157, 179) sts.

NEXT ROW: Work Row 1 of Right Front chart over first 34 (45, 56, 67) sts and dec them to 33 (44, 55, 66) sts as shown on chart, pm, [k1, p1] 4 times, [k1, p1, k2tog, p1, k1, p2tog, k1, p1] 3 times, [k1, p1] 3 times, k1, pm, work Row 1 of left front chart over last 34 (45, 56, 67) sts and dec them to 33 (44, 55, 66) sts as shown on chart—105 (127, 149, 171) sts.

Working center 39 sts between m in seed st (see Stitch Guide), work Rows 2–4 of front charts once, rep Rows 5–8 of charts 5 (5, 6, 6) times, then work Rows 9–11 of charts once, ending with a RS row—87 (87, 91, 91) rows total from beg; piece measures about 17½ (17½, 18¼, 18¼)″ (44.5 [44.5, 46.5, 46.5] cm) from CO. Do not cut yarn. Place sts on holder.

LEFT FRONT EDGING

With RS facing, yarn attached at end of left front sts, and size 9 (5.5 mm) cir needle, pick up and knit 59 (59, 61, 61) sts along left front selvedge. Work 1 WS row in seed st. Work short-rows to shape lower edge as foll:

SHORT-ROW 1: (RS) Work 56 (56, 58, 58) sts in patt, turn.

SHORT-ROWS 2, 4, 6, and 8: (WS) Yo, work in patt to end.

SHORT-ROW 3: Work 52 (52, 54, 54) sts in patt, turn.

SHORT-ROW 5: Work 48 (48, 50, 50) sts in patt, turn.

SHORT-ROW 7: Work 44 (44, 46, 46) sts in patt, turn.

SHORT-ROW 9: *Work in patt to yo, work yo tog with st after it as k2tog or p2tog to maintain seed st patt; rep from * 3 more times, work in patt to end.

Work 1 WS row in seed st across all sts—piece measures about 1¾" (4.5 cm) from pick-up row at neck edge (beg of RS rows) and ½" (1.3 cm) from pick-up row at lower edge (end of RS rows). Place sts on holder.

RIGHT FRONT EDGING

With RS facing, size 9 (5.5 mm) cir needle, and beg at lower corner of right front, pick up and knit 59 (59, 61, 61) sts along right front selvedge. Work 2 rows in seed st, ending with a RS row. Beg with Short-row 1 as a WS row, work Short-rows 1–9 as for left front edging, ending with Short-row 9 as a WS row—piece measures about 1¾" (4.5 cm) from pick-up row at neck edge (end of RS rows) and ½" (1.3 cm) from pick-up row at lower edge (beg of RS rows). Place sts on holder.

Yoke

JOIN BODY AND SLEEVES

Return 105 (127, 149, 171) held lower body sts to size 9 (5.5 mm) 36" (90 cm) cir needle and join yarn with RS facing to last row of right front edging.

JOINING ROW: Pick up and knit 11 sts across selvedge of edging alternating picking up as if to knit and as if to purl to imitate seed st patt, and beg and ending by picking up as if to knit. Cont in established seed st patt, work 17 (22, 27, 31) right front sts, temporarily sl next st to right needle, place the foll 10 (10, 12, 14) sts on holder for right underarm, place 40 (40, 48, 56) held right sleeve sts on left needle, return slipped st to left needle and work it tog with the first sleeve st as ssk and hang a removable marker in the st itself (not on the needle between sts), work next 38 (38, 46, 54) sleeve sts in seed st, work last sleeve st tog with st after it as k2tog and hang a removable marker in the st itself, work 47 (59, 67, 77) sts in seed st for back, temporarily sl next st to right needle, place the foll 10 (10, 12, 14) sts on holder for left underarm, place 40 (40, 48, 56) held left sleeve sts on left needle, return slipped st to left needle and work it tog with the first sleeve st as ssk and hang a removable marker in the st itself (not on the needle between sts), work next 38 (38, 46, 54) sleeve sts in seed st, work last sleeve st tog with st after it as k2tog and hang a removable marker in the st itself, work 17 (22, 27, 31) left front sts, pick up and knit 11 sts across selvedge of left front edging alternating picking up as if to knit and as if to purl—183 (205, 239, 273) sts total; 4 marked raglan sts; 38 (38, 46, 54) sts each sleeve; 28 (33, 38, 42) sts each front; 47 (59, 67, 77) back sts.

NEXT ROW: (WS) *Work in patt to marked raglan st, purl marked st; rep from * 3 more times, work in patt to end.

SEED STITCH LOWER YOKE

Change to size 8 (5 mm) 36" (90 cm) cir needle. For this section, maintain seed st patt between marked raglan sts and work marked sts in St st, moving markers up as you work so you can always easily identify these sts.

DEC ROW: (RS) *Work in patt to 2 sts before marked st, work k2tog or p2tog as necessary to maintain patt, knit marked st, work ssk or ssp as necessary to maintain patt; rep from * 3 more times, work in patt to end—8 sts dec'd; 2 sts from each sleeve and back; 1 st from each front.

NEXT ROW: (WS) *Work in patt to marked raglan st, purl marked st; rep from * 3 more times, work in patt to end.

Rep the last 2 rows 4 (4, 5, 6) more times—143 (165, 191, 217) sts rem; 4 marked raglan sts; 28 (28, 34, 40) sts each sleeve; 23 (28, 32, 35) sts each front; 37 (49, 55, 63) back sts; yoke measures about 1¾ (1¾, 2¼, 2½)" (4.5 [4.5, 5.5, 6.5] cm) from joining row. Work short-rows to raise center back neck while cont raglan decs as foll:

SHORT-ROW 1: (RS) *Work in patt to 2 sts before marked st, work k2tog or p2tog as required, knit marked st, work ssk or ssp as required; rep from * once more, work in patt to 2 sts before marked left back raglan st, turn—4 sts dec'd; 2 sts from right sleeve; 1 st each at right front and right back raglans.

SHORT-ROW 2: (WS) Yo, work in patt to 2 sts before marked right back raglan st, turn.

SHORT-ROW 3: Yo, work in patt to 2 sts before yo at previous turning point, turn.

SHORT-ROWS 4, 5, AND 6: Rep Row 3.

SHORT-ROW 7: [Work in patt to yo, work yo tog with st after it as k2tog or p2tog] 3 times, *work k2tog or p2tog over 2 sts before marked st as required, knit marked raglan st, work ssk or ssp as required,* work in patt to 2 sts before next marked st, rep from * to * once more, work in patt to end—4 sts dec'd; 2 sts from left sleeve; 1 st each at left back and front raglans.

SHORT-ROW 8: [Work in patt to marked raglan st, purl marked st] 2 times, [work in patt to yo, work yo tog with st after it as ssk or p2tog] 3 times, [work in patt to marked raglan st, purl

marked st] 2 times, work in patt to end—135 (157, 183, 209) sts;
4 marked raglan sts; 26 (26, 32, 38) sts each sleeve; 22 (27, 31,
34) sts each front; 35 (47, 53, 61) back sts; yoke measures about
3 (3, 3¹/₂, 3³/₄)" (7.5 [7.5, 9, 9.5] cm) from joining row at center
back and 2 (2, 2¹/₂, 2³/₄)" (5 [5, 6.5, 7] cm) from joining row at
front selvedges.

[Work the dec row, then work 1 WS row even] 2 (4, 7, 11) times,
then work the dec row once more to end with a RS row—111 (117,
119, 113) sts rem; 4 marked raglan sts; 20 (16, 16, 14) sts each
sleeve; 19 (22, 23, 22) sts each front; 29 (37, 37, 37) back sts; yoke
measures about 3³/₄ (4¹/₄, 5³/₄, 7¹/₄)" (9.5 [11, 14.5, 18.5] cm) from
joining row at center back and 2³/₄ (3¹/₄, 4³/₄, 6¹/₄)" (7 [8.5, 12,
16] cm) from joining row at front selvedges. Purl 1 WS row, inc 3
(dec 3, dec 5, inc 1) st(s) evenly spaced—114 sts for all sizes.

SPIRAL PATTERN UPPER YOKE

Work Rows 1–20 of Yoke chart—79 sts; chart section measures
about 3³/₄" (9.5 cm) from end of seed st lower yoke; entire yoke
measures about 7¹/₂ (8, 9¹/₂, 11)" (19 [20.5, 24, 28] cm) from
joining row at center back and 6¹/₂ (7, 8¹/₂, 10)" (16.5 [18, 21.5,
25.5 cm) from joining row at front selvedges. Place sts on holder.

Finishing

Block to measurements.

COLLAR

Place 79 held yoke sts on size 7 (4.5 mm) cir needle and rejoin
yarn with RS facing.

NEXT ROW: (RS) Work in seed st, dec 4 sts evenly spaced—75
sts rem.

Work 9 rows even in seed st, beg and ending with a WS row.
Work short-rows to shape collar as foll:

SHORT-ROW 1: (RS) Work 57 sts in patt, turn.

SHORT-ROW 2: (WS) Yo, work 39 sts in patt, turn.

SHORT-ROW 3: Yo, work in patt to yo, work yo tog with st after it as
k2tog or p2tog to maintain seed-st patt, work 2 sts in patt, turn.

SHORT-ROWS 4–6: Rep Short-row 3.

SHORT-ROW 7: Yo, work in patt to yo, work yo tog with st after
it as k2tog or p2tog, work in patt to end.

SHORT-ROW 8: Work in patt to yo, work yo tog with st after it
as k2tog or p2tog, work in patt to end—75 sts; all yo's have been

worked; collar measures 3″ (7.5 cm) high at center back and 2¼″ (5.5 cm) at front selvedges.

Cut yarn and leave sts on needle. To reinforce base of collar and prevent it from stretching, join yarn with WS facing to left front edge aligned with first row of collar. Using a crochet hook, work a row of sl st crochet (see Glossary) firmly and invisibly along WS of first collar row, working about 7 sl sts for every 8 sts of collar. Fasten off.

FRONT BIND-OFF

Place 59 (59, 61, 61) held sts of right front on size 7 (4.5 mm) 36″ (90 cm) cir needle and rejoin yarn to lower corner of right front with RS facing. Work across 59 (59, 61, 61) right front sts in es-tablished seed st patt, pick up and knit 36 (39, 47, 56) sts along right front selvedge of yoke and collar, picking up as if to knit or as if to purl alternately to maintain patt, work across 75 collar sts in patt, pick up and knit 36 (39, 47, 56) sts along left front sel-vedge of collar and yoke, picking up alternately as before, return 59 (59, 61, 61) held left front sts to needle and work across them in patt—265 (271, 291, 309) sts total. With WS facing, work picot BO as foll: K2, BO 1 st, *sl st on right needle after BO back to left needle, use the cable method to CO 1 st, k2, BO 1 st, [k1, BO 1 st] 2 times;* rep from * to * along left front and seed st section of yoke, then use the decrease method (see Glossary) to BO sts along the spiral section of left front yoke, around the collar, and along spiral section of right front yoke; change back to picot BO and rep from * to * along right front seed st section of yoke and along right front. Fasten off last st.

With yarn threaded on a tapestry needle, use the Kitchener st (see Glossary) to graft body and sleeves at underarms. Weave in loose ends. Block again, if desired.

STELLA

CYBÈLE ✳ *lace-up tank*

My husband and I initially chose Cybèle for our daughter's name, much to the horror of his mother, who wanted no grandchild of hers associated with a heathen goddess of the rowdy bacchanals of early Roman mythology. We decided on something more conventional—we called her Rain.

I have always tried to imagine what Cybèle would have worn (surely not the usual flowing goddess robes). In this French Alps–inspired garment, the look is more mountains than Mediterranean. Asymmetrical styling, easy-to-work cables, and a caramel-hued organic yarn from one of my favorite merchants (Daphne, at The Fibre Company) make Cybèle *un modèle rapide*. Wear this top piously laced up over a cotton dress for autumn or more adventurously, with little (or nothing) underneath. Add a leather skirt, tall boots, and go forth and revel.

FINISHED SIZE

31 (34, 37, 40, 43)" (78.5 [86.5, 94, 101.5, 109] cm) bust circumference with front edges touching when laced together; front lacing can be loosened to accommodate larger or in-between sizes. Vest shown measures 31" (78.5 cm).

YARN

Worsted weight (#4 Medium).

SHOWN HERE: The Fibre Company Terra (60% merino, 20% baby alpaca, 20% silk; 100 yd [91 ml/50 g): chestnut, 5 (5, 6, 7, 7) skeins.

NEEDLES

BODY AND STRAPS: size U.S. 9 (5.5 mm). STRAP PICKUP: size U.S. 7 (4.5 mm). *Adjust needle size if necessary to obtain the correct gauge.*

NOTIONS

Stitch holders or waste yarn for holders; tapestry needle; three ⅝" (1.6 cm) buttons.

GAUGE

16 stitches and 20 rows = 4" (10 cm) in reverse stockinette stitch on larger needles; 33 stitches and 24 rows (3 pattern repeats wide and 3 pattern repeats high) = 6¾" (17 cm) wide and 4½" (11.5 cm) high in diagonal cable patterns on larger needles, after blocking.

Notes

- The body is made up of two different-size cable panels, which will naturally form parallelograms because of the bias effect of the cable patterns.
- The finished vest is assembled with the cables running from side to side. The panels are held together in the front by off-center lacing and in the back by an asymmetrical button closure.
- The finished bust measurement is equal to the lengths of both panels along the upper body selvedge, less 3½" (9 cm) for the overlap of the back button closure.
- The different-length reverse-stockinette straps are grafted to the upper edge of the body using Kitchener stitch. Finished right armhole measures about 7 (7¼, 7½, 8, 8½)" (18 [18.5, 19, 20.5, 21.5] cm) high; finished left armhole measures about 7½ (7¾, 8, 8½, 9)" (19 [19.5, 20.5, 21.5, 23] cm) high.

Stitch Guide

C6B *(WORKED WITHOUT A CABLE NEEDLE)*

Skip the first 3 sts on left needle, insert right needle tip into the front of the next 3 sts on left needle, slip all 6 sts off left needle (first 3 sts will temporarily be loose behind the needles), insert the right needle tip into the 3 loose sts from right to left—all 6 sts rearranged on right needle as for a right-crossing cable. Transfer all 6 sts back to left needle and knit them in their new order to complete the cable.

C6F *(WORKED WITHOUT A CABLE NEEDLE)*

Skip the first 3 sts on left needle, insert right needle tip into the back of the next 3 sts on left needle, slip all 6 sts off left needle (first 3 sts will temporarily be loose in front of the needles), insert the right needle tip into the 3 loose sts from right to left—all 6 sts rearranged on right needle as for a left-crossing cable. Transfer all 6 sts back to left needle and knit them in their new order to complete the cable.

Left Panel

Using a provisional method (see Glossary), CO 65 (65, 76, 76, 76) sts.

ROWS 1, 3, AND 7: (RS) Sl 1 pwise with yarn in back (wyb), k2tog, yo, *k6, k2tog, k3, yo; rep from * to last 7 sts, k7.

ROWS 2, 4, AND 6: Sl 1 pwise with yarn in front (wyf), purl to end.

ROW 5: Sl 1 pwise wyb, k2tog, yo, *C6B (see Stitch Guide), k2tog, k3, yo; rep from * to last 7 sts, C6B, k1.

ROW 8: Sl 1 pwise wyf, purl to end.

Work Rows 1–8 a total of 12 (13, 14, 15, 16) times—96 (104, 112, 120, 128) patt rows completed. BO all sts.

Right Panel

Using a provisional method, CO 65 (65, 76, 76, 76) sts.

ROWS 1, 3, and 7: (RS) Sl 1 pwise wyb, k6, *yo, k3, ssk, k6; *rep from * to last 3 sts, yo, k2tog, k1.

ROWS 2, 4, and 6: Sl 1 pwise wyf, purl to end.

ROW 5: Sl 1 pwise wyb, C6F (see Stitch Guide), *yo, k3, ssk, C6F; rep from * to last 3 sts, yo, k2tog, k1.

ROW 8: Sl 1 pwise wyf, purl to end.

Work Rows 1–8 a total of 11 (12, 13, 14, 15) times—88 (96, 104, 112, 120) patt rows completed. BO all sts.

Shoulder Straps

RIGHT STRAP

Using a provisional method, CO 15 sts. (NOTE: CO edge of strap will be attached to the upper back of the garment during finishing.) Beg with a RS purl row, work in rev St st (purl RS rows; knit WS rows) for 2 rows.

DEC ROW: (RS) P2tog, purl to end—1 st dec'd at armhole edge of strap.

Knit 1 WS row, then rep dec row once more—13 sts rem. Work even in rev St st until piece measures 13 (13½, 14, 15, 16)" (33 [34.5, 35.5, 38, 40.5] cm) from CO, or about 1" (2.5 cm) less than desired total length, ending with a WS row. Place sts on holder.

LEFT STRAP

Using a provisional method. CO 15 sts. Beg with a RS purl row, work in rev St st for 2 rows.

DEC ROW: (RS) Purl to last 2 sts, ssp (see Glossary)—1 st dec'd at armhole edge of strap.

Knit 1 WS row, then rep the dec row once more—13 sts rem. Work even in rev St st until piece measures 14 (14½, 15, 16, 17)" (35.5 [37, 38, 40.5, 43] cm) from CO, or about 1" (2.5) less than desired total length, ending with a WS row. Place sts on holder.

NOTE: Left strap is deliberately 1" (2.5 cm) longer than right strap because the asymmetrical back closure pulls the right back higher than the left back, making the left armhole about ½" (1.3 cm) deeper than the right armhole.

Finishing

Wet-block cable panels into parallelogram shapes as shown on schematic. Block straps to about 3" (7.5 cm) wide at CO edge, and allow strap selvedges to roll gently toward the purled RS so straps measure about 2¼" (5.5 cm) wide at center with edges rolled.

FRONT LACING

Cut 2 strands of yarn, each about 6 (6, 6½, 6½, 6½) yd (5.5 [5.5, 6, 6, 6] m) long, or about 4½ times the desired finished cord length. Hold strands tog and fold in half to form two groups of 2 strands each. Anchor the strands at the fold by looping them over a doorknob. Holding one group in each hand, twist each group tightly in a clockwise direction until they begin to kink. Put both groups in one hand, then release them, allowing them

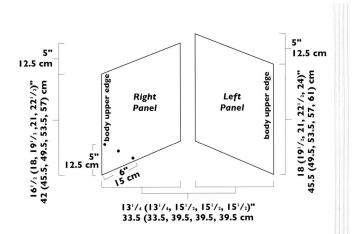

5"
12.5 cm

5"
12.5 cm

*body upper edge

Right Panel

Left Panel

body upper edge

16½ (18, 19½, 21, 22⅔)"
42 (45.5, 49.5, 53.5, 57) cm

5"
12.5 cm

6"
15 cm

18 (19½, 21, 22½, 24)"
45.5 (49.5, 53.5, 57, 61) cm

13¼ (13¼, 15½, 15½, 15½)"
33.5 (33.5, 39.5, 39.5, 39.5 cm

BACK BUTTON CLOSURE

With RS facing, mark positions for three buttons near CO edge of right panel, the highest centered on last cable column at end of RS rows and 5″ (12.5 cm) up from CO edge, and the lowest close to CO edge and about 6″ (15 cm) before end of RS rows. Lay a ruler along these two marked button positions and mark the third button position exactly in the center of the line connecting the first two buttons; approximate positions of buttons are indicated by dots on schematic. Temporarily pin or tie buttons to marked positions. Lay garment on flat surface with WS of laced front facing up and selvedges with [yo, k2tog] eyelets at the top. Fold right back in toward center, then fold left back inward to overlap right back. Button each button through eyelets closest to CO edge of left panel, with the top button through eyelet at upper selvedge of left panel and the rem two buttons through the next two eyelet columns between cables on left panel.

STRAPS

Lay garment flat with back of assembled body facing upward. Temporarily pin CO edge of right strap to upper edge of right back so inner (neck) edge of strap is about 5″ (12.5 cm) from CO edge of right panel and aligned over top button. Temporarily pin CO edge of left strap to upper edge of left back so neck edge of strap is about 3½″ (9 cm) from CO edge of left panel. Turn garment over and temporarily pin ends of straps with held sts to upper edges of fronts, with neck edge of right front strap about 1 (1½, 2, 2½, 3)″ (2.5 [3.8, 5, 6.5, 7.5] cm) from BO edge of right panel and neck edge of left strap about 4 (4½, 5, 5½, 6)″ (10 [11.5, 12.5, 14, 15] cm) from BO edge of left panel. Armhole edges of straps will be about 4½ (5½, 6½, 7½, 8½)″ (11.5 [14, 16.5, 19, 21.5] cm) apart. Try on garment and evaluate the fit; armhole height should be a bit snug with straps slightly stretched because finishing the straps will add 5 rows (about 1″ [2.5 cm]) to the length of each strap.

Right Strap

Return 13 held right strap sts to needles and rejoin yarn with RS facing. Add or remove rows in rev St st if necessary until strap is about 1″ (2.5 cm) shorter than desired length.

INC ROW: (RS) P1, M1 (see Glossary), purl to end—1 st inc'd at armhole edge of strap.

Knit 1 WS row, then rep the inc row once more—15 sts. Work 2 rows even in rev St st—strap measures about 14 (14½, 15, 16, 17)″

to twist around each other counterclockwise. Smooth out the twists so that they are uniform along the length of the cord. Trim cord to about 48 (48, 52½, 52½, 52½)″ (122 [122, 133.5, 133.5, 133.5] cm) long and tie an overhand knot about 1½″ (3.8 cm) from each end. Lay cable panels RS up on flat surface with BO ends of panels touching and panel selvedges with [yo, k2tog] eyelets at the top. Beg at upper edge, lace BO edges tog by threading cord back and forth, shoelace-fashion, through eyelets along BO edges of panels, leaving the lowest eyelets free on each side. Draw up cord until front edges meet.

(35.5 [37, 38, 40.5, 43] cm) or desired adjusted length. With smaller needles, RS facing, and beg 1 (1½, 2, 2½, 3)" (2.5 [3.8, 5, 6.5, 7.5] cm) from BO edge of right panel, pick up and knit 15 sts from next 8 slipped selvedge sts along upper edge of right front. With yarn threaded on a tapestry needle, use the Kitchener st (see Glossary) to join live strap sts to picked-up front sts. With smaller needles, RS facing, and beg 8" (20.5 cm) from CO edge of right panel, pick up and knit 15 sts from next 8 slipped selvedge sts along upper edge of right back, ending about 5" (12.5 cm) from CO end of right panel. Carefully remove provisional CO from base of strap sts and place 15 exposed sts on smaller needle. Use the Kitchener st to join picked-up body sts to base of provisional CO strap sts.

Left Strap
Return 13 held left strap sts to needles and rejoin yarn with RS facing. Add or remove rows in rev St st if necessary until strap is about 1" (2.5 cm) shorter than desired length.

INC ROW: (RS) Purl to last st, M1, p1—1 st inc'd at armhole edge of strap.

Knit 1 WS row, then rep the inc row once more—15 sts. Work 2 rows even in rev St st—strap measures about 15 (15½, 16, 17, 18)" (38 [39.5, 40.5, 43, 45.5] cm) or desired adjusted length. With smaller needles, RS facing, and beg about 7 (7½, 8, 8½, 9)" (18 [19, 20.5, 21.5, 23] cm) from BO edge of left panel, pick up and knit 15 sts from next 8 slipped selvedge sts along upper edge of left front, ending about 4 (4½, 5, 5½, 6)" (10 [11.5, 12.5, 14, 15] cm) from BO edge of left panel. Use the Kitchener st to join live strap sts to picked-up front sts. With smaller needles, RS facing, and beg about 3½" (9 cm) from CO edge of left panel, pick up and knit 15 sts from next 8 slipped selvedge sts along upper edge of left back. Carefully remove provisional CO from base of strap sts and place 15 exposed sts on smaller needle. Use the Kitchener st to join picked-up body sts to base of provisional CO strap sts.

Join Right Back to Side of Left Strap
With RS facing, carefully remove provisional CO from 8 sts closest to upper edge of right panel and place exposed sts on smaller needle. With RS facing, smaller needle, and beg where left strap meets upper back, pick up and knit 8 sts along neck edge of left strap. Use the Kitchener st to join sts picked up from side of strap to base of provisional CO right panel sts.

Carefully remove waste yarn from provisional CO of rem sts of right panel, place sts on larger needle, then use the decrease method (see Glossary) to BO rem sts. Carefully remove waste yarn from provisional CO of left panel, place all sts on larger needle, then use the decrease method to BO all sts. Sew buttons permanently in place, adjusting final positions as necessary. Weave in loose ends. Lightly block again if desired to neaten back edges. Adjust front lacing for desired fit and tie ends of cord at bottom.

ONDINE ✳ *appliquéd skirt*

For me, designing a knitted skirt involves equal parts desire and dismay. I love the concept but fear the challenge of finding a yarn that will not let me down (literally). I picture the rear view of some failed attempts: not a pretty sight! Enter fulling—a meeting of wool, hot water, and friction—and voilà, a fabric is transformed. A wonderfully alive and naturally produced yarn from my neighbor Leanne of Beaverslide Dry Goods in Montana came to the rescue. This yarn practically leapt into the soapy bath by itself, and the resulting metamorphosis encouraged me to believe that, even with wear, Ondine would behave herself.

Purled stitches, lightly fulled, yielded a most satisfying texture, and the rough-hewn nature of the garment was further reinforced by the leaf appliqués and the decidedly naïve stitchery at the edges. Short-rows and side-to-side construction gave me a basic blueprint for the curvy shape I was seeking. Closures can be whatever you fancy, and you can easily adjust the length by casting on extra stitches (based on your post-fulled gauge swatch).

FINISHED SIZE

35½ (38, 41, 44, 47, 50)" (90 [96.5, 104, 112, 119.5, 127] cm) hip circumference measured about 5" (12.5 cm) down from finished upper edge, 28 (31, 34, 36½, 39½, 42½)" (71 [78.5, 86.5, 92.5, 100.5, 108] cm) waist circumference, and about 18½" (47 cm) long, after fulling and hemming. Skirt shown measures about 35½" (90 cm) at the hip. NOTE: The amount of front overlap can be adjusted to accommodate slightly smaller, larger, or in-between sizes.

YARN

Worsted weight (#4 Medium) for main color and light sportweight (#2 Fine) for embellishment.

SHOWN HERE: Beaverslide Dry Goods Worsted Weight 2-Ply (65% merino, 35% kid mohair; 210 yd [192 m]/4 oz [113 g]): mink (MC), (3, 3, 3, 4, 4) skeins.

Rowan Kid Classic (70% lambswool, 26% kid mohair, 4% nylon; 153 yd [140 m]/50 g): #832 peat (dark brown, CC1), 1 skein.

Beaverslide Dry Goods Light Sport Weight (90% merino, 10% kid mohair; 440 yd [402 m]/4 oz [113 g]): chokecherry heather (rose; CC2), 1 skein.

NEEDLES

SKIRT: size U.S. 9 (5.5 mm): 36" (90 cm) circular (cir). PROVISIONAL CAST-ON: size U.S. 8 (5 mm): straight. Leaves—size U.S. 5 (3.75 mm): straight. *Adjust needle size if necessary to obtain the correct gauge.*

NOTIONS

Size H/8 (5 mm) crochet hook; markers (m); stitch holders; sewing pins; tapestry needle; decorative pin for fastening skirt.

GAUGE

16 stitches and 22 rows = 4" (10 cm) in reverse stockinette with MC with largest needle, after fulling.

Notes

- The skirt is worked in one piece from side to side, beginning with a provisional cast-on at left back, then working across the back with short-rows to shape the right hip, and continuing to the right front edge. Stitches from the provisional back cast-on are then returned to the needle, the left hip short-row shaping is worked, then the left front is worked to end at the left front edge.
- To customize length, begin by casting on more or fewer stitches. Every 4 stitches added or removed will lengthen or shorten the skirt by about 1" (2.5 cm). For a longer skirt, plan on purchasing extra yarn.
- The schematic shows the skirt measurements after fulling but before hemming and embellishment. The skirt is lightly fulled—not felted—to the dimensions shown. The stitches and rows of the fulled fabric should still be clearly visible and distinct.
- During finishing the hemmed edges are secured with running stitches. The appliquéd leaves are cut from a rectangle of contrasting-color fulled fabric and appliquéd to the right front as shown, then the embroidered stem and leaf details are added.

Skirt

BACK

With crochet hook and medium-size needle, use the crochet-on method (see Glossary) to provisionally CO 80 sts (see Notes for length adjustments). Change to largest needles and MC. Beg with a RS purl row, work in rev St st (purl RS rows; knit WS rows) for 74 (82, 90, 98, 106, 114) rows, ending with a WS row.

SHAPE RIGHT BACK HIP

Work short-rows using the yarnover method to close the gaps as foll:

SHORT-ROW 1: (RS) Purl to last 15 sts, place marker (pm), turn.

SHORT-ROWS 2, 4, 6, 8, AND 10: (WS) Yo, knit to end.

SHORT-ROW 3: Purl to 3 sts before m (counting the turning yarnover as 1 st), turn.

SHORT-ROW 5: Purl to 6 sts before m (counting all yarnovers), turn.

SHORT-ROW 7: Purl to 9 sts before m (counting all yarnovers), turn.

SHORT-ROW 9: Purl to 12 sts before m (counting all yarnovers), turn.

SHORT-ROW 11: *Purl to yo, work yo tog with st after it as p2tog; rep from * 4 more times, purl to end.

RIGHT FRONT

Work 3 rows even in rev St st, beg and ending with a WS row. Work Short-rows 1–11 as for right back hip, ending with a RS row. Work 69 (73, 77, 81, 85, 89) rows in rev St st, beg and ending with a WS row. BO all sts.

SHAPE LEFT BACK HIP

Carefully remove waste yarn from provisional CO at beg of back and place 80 exposed sts on largest needle. Join yarn at hem edge with WS (knit side) of back facing. Work short-rows as foll:

SHORT-ROW 1: (WS) Knit to last 15 sts, pm, turn.

SHORT-ROWS 2, 4, 6, 8, AND 10: (RS) Yo, purl to end.

SHORT-ROW 3: Knit to 3 sts before m (counting yarnover), turn.

SHORT-ROW 5: Knit to 6 sts before m (counting all yarnovers), turn.

SHORT-ROW 7: Knit to 9 sts before m (counting all yarnovers), turn.

SHORT-ROW 9: Knit to 12 sts before m (counting all yarnovers), turn.

SHORT-ROW 11: *Knit to yo, work yo tog with st after it as ssk; rep from * 4 more times, knit to end.

LEFT FRONT

Work 3 rows even in rev St st, beg and ending with a RS row. Work Short-rows 1–11 as for left back hip, ending with a WS row. Work 48 (52, 56, 60, 64, 68) rows in rev St st, ending with a WS row. BO all sts.

Fulling

Weave in loose ends. Fill a sink or tub with hot water and about 1 teaspoon of shampoo or mild liquid soap. Squeeze garment in water for about 3 to 5 minutes until fabric is lightly fulled to gauge (individual sts will still be visible). NOTE: Fulling in the washing machine is not recommended; doing so may cause the fabric to felt too much. Rinse, then squeeze out excess water, being careful not to stretch or wring the fabric. Lay skirt flat, straighten the edges, pin in place to measurements shown on schematic, and allow to air-dry thoroughly.

Finishing

WAIST, HEM, AND FRONT EDGES

Fold about 3/4" (2 cm) toward the RS (purl side) of skirt along selvedges at waist and lower edge and pin in place. Carefully steam to set the fold lines. With CC1 threaded on a tapestry needle, work running sts (see Glossary) about 3/8" (1 cm) long and 3/8" (1 cm) apart along both edges as shown to hem waist and lower edge. Fold about 1/2" (1.3 cm) toward the WS (knit side) of the skirt along BO edge of right front, pin in place, and carefully steam fold line. With CC1 threaded on a tapestry needle, work 3/8" (1 cm) running sts to secure right front edge finish as shown. With RS facing, measure down about 10" (25.5 cm) from finished waist edge along BO edge of left front and make a 1/2" (1.3 cm) snip in the fabric (fulled fabric will not ravel). Fold BO edge of left front below the snip about 1/2" (1.3 cm) to the WS (knit side) of the skirt, pin in place, and carefully steam. With CC1 threaded on a tapestry needle, work 3/8" (1 cm) running sts to secure left front edge below the snip as shown.

LEAVES AND EMBROIDERY

With CC2 and smallest needle, CO 30 sts. Work in St st for 70 rows. Loosely BO all sts. Full fabric as directed above, but for a few more minutes so the sts are slightly more blurred than in the main skirt fabric. Cut 9 assorted leaf shapes ranging in size from 2" (5 cm) to 3 1/2" (9 cm) long from fulled CC2 piece. Pin leaves in place on right front, cascading down from the waist as shown in photograph. With CC1 threaded on a tapestry needle, attach leaves by working 1/4" (0.6 cm) straight sts radiating out from the center around all sides of each leaf as shown. Work veins along the center of leaves as desired using CC1 and small running stitches. With CC1 and using a stem stitch (see Glossary), work stems connecting leaves as shown.

Fasten with decorative pin.

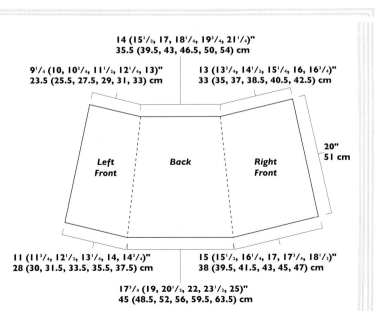

14 (15 1/2, 17, 18 1/4, 19 3/4, 21 1/4)"
35.5 (39.5, 43, 46.5, 50, 54) cm

9 1/4 (10, 10 3/4, 11 1/2, 12 1/4, 13)"
23.5 (25.5, 27.5, 29, 31, 33) cm

13 (13 3/4, 14 1/2, 15 1/4, 16, 16 3/4)"
33 (35, 37, 38.5, 40.5, 42.5) cm

Left Front   Back   Right Front

20"
51 cm

11 (11 3/4, 12 1/2, 13 1/4, 14, 14 3/4)"
28 (30, 31.5, 33.5, 35.5, 37.5) cm

15 (15 1/2, 16 1/4, 17, 17 3/4, 18 1/2)"
38 (39.5, 41.5, 43, 45, 47) cm

17 3/4 (19, 20 1/2, 22, 23 1/2, 25)"
45 (48.5, 52, 56, 59.5, 63.5) cm

la CRÉATRICE

INNOVATIVE AND UNCONVENTIONAL

Creative thinking and improvisation ran hot in my childhood home, spurred on by my parents' encouragement to "make something out of nothing." When I learned to sew as a girl, I discovered the feeling of empowerment that comes when the cosmic creativity switch gets flipped to the permanent "on" position. One exciting endeavor followed the next and I, *la créatrice*, spent hours devouring a constantly expanding shelf of how-to books on every subject—from playing guitar and piano to embroidering to hand-tooling leather.

France has a storied history of incubating creative minds, from Vincent Van Gogh to Colette, James Baldwin, and Camille Claudel. La Créatrice brings together my personal homage to favorite French artistic icons with my excitement about experimenting with unfamiliar techniques. Just by picking up your knitting and choosing to learn something new, you reinforce your "creative gene." I love the way knitting challenges us to develop an ever-expanding repertoire of skills as well as the way our confidence increases when we modify a pattern to suit our own personality. The design process continues to surprise me: an unexpected "accident" or "mistake" might lead to a serendipitous outcome. Trust, follow, and create, my lovelies!

DELPHINE * *lacy cap-sleeve top*

"When in France, let us be adventuresome in our menu choices,"* I reminded my husband as we settled into a cozy *ferme-auberge* perched high above the Mediterranean. To that end, we happily ordered *casserole de ecrevisse*, thinking it to be a first-course casserole of mouthwatering shrimp. We had completely forgotten that the word *casserole* means "saucepan," and *ecrevisse* didn't mean "shrimp." What we got was a dish of scrawny, barely dead crayfish with hardly a morsel of flesh on them. We were saved by the copious cheese course, which introduced us to what became a new favorite: freshly made local goat cheese with chestnut honey. Good things can emerge from near misadventures. The design for Delphine is a case in point.

Delphine almost ended up on the cutting room floor when, at the eleventh hour, I boldly chopped off the entire top third. Thankfully, from this little casserole of pale shrimp-pink yarn ends, something new and better did emerge—a modern lace corset fashioned from hem to neckline in dreamy alpaca silk with tiny picot edges. It was good indeed to be reminded that although initial plans may go awry, creative solutions are never far if we have faith. Indeed, "All's well that ends well"!

FINISHED SIZE

27½ (35¼, 43)" (70 [89.5, 109] cm) bust circumference. Sweater shown measures 35¼" (89.5 cm). NOTE: Fabric can be stretched and blocked wider to accommodate sizes up to 3" (7.5 cm) larger.

YARN

Sportweight (#2 Fine).

SHOWN HERE: Blue Sky Alpacas Alpaca Silk (50% alpaca, 50% silk; 146 yd [133 ml/50 g]: #133 blush, 3 (4, 5) skeins.

NEEDLES

BODY: sizes U.S. 2, 3, and 4 (2.75, 3.25, and 3.5 mm): 24" and 36" (60 and 90 cm) circular (cir). NECK EDGING: size U.S. 2 (3 mm) 16" and 36" (40 and 90 cm) cir. PROVISIONAL CAST-ON: size U.S. 4 (3.5 mm): straight. *Adjust needle size if necessary to obtain the correct gauge.*

NOTIONS

Tapestry needle; markers (m); stitch holders; size F/5 (3.75 mm) crochet hook; three ¼" (6 mm) pearl buttons; 1½ yds (1.25 m) ¼" (6 mm) silk ribbon.

GAUGE

21 stitches and 32 rows/rounds (3 repeats wide and 8 repeats high) of lacy stripe pattern measure 5" (12.5 cm) wide and 4½" (11.5 cm) high on size 3 (3.25 mm) needle; 27 stitches of lower edge pattern (3 repeats) measure 5¾" (14.5 cm) wide on size 4 (3.5 mm) needle; 33 stitches (three 11-stitch repeats) of front bodice pattern Rnds 13–20 measure 6¾" (17 cm) wide on size 3 (3.25 mm) needle; 17 stitches and 27 rows = 4" (10 cm) in upper bodice pattern on size 2 (2.75 mm) needle.

Notes

The lower body is worked in the round to the armholes, then divided for working the fronts and back separately back and forth in rows. Variations of the vertical lacy stripes pattern that contain more stockinette stitches are used at the lower edge for shaping and on the front bodice to provide more modest coverage. The upper bodice and straps are knitted in an openwork lace pattern and the live stitches of the straps are grafted together at the shoulders.

To customize lower body length, repeat Rounds 17–20 of front bodice pattern more or fewer times before dividing for the upper body. Every 4 rounds added or removed will lengthen or shorten the lower body by about ½" (1.3 cm).

Stitch Guide

LOWER EDGE PATTERN *(MULTIPLE OF 9 STS)*

RND 1: *P2, k1tbl, p2, [k2tog, yo] 2 times; rep from *.

RNDS 2 AND 4: *P2, k1tbl, p2, k4; rep from *

RND 3: *P2, k1tbl, p2, [yo, ssk] 2 times; rep from *.

Repeat Rnds 1–4 for pattern.

LACY STRIPE PATTERN *(MULTIPLE OF 7 STS)*

RND 1: *P1, k1tbl, p1, [k2tog, yo] 2 times; rep from *.

RNDS 2 AND 4: *P1, k1tbl, p1, k4; rep from *.

RND 3: *P1, k1tbl, p1, [yo, ssk] 2 times; rep from *.

Repeat Rnds 1–4 for pattern.

FRONT BODICE PATTERN
(MULTIPLE OF 7 STS, INC TO MULTIPLE OF 11 STS)

RND 1: *P1, M1P (see Glossary), k1tbl, M1P, p1, [k2tog, yo] 2 times; rep from *—patt rep has inc'd to a multiple of 9 sts.

RNDS 2, 4, 6, 8, 10, AND 12: *P2, k1tbl, p2, k4; rep from *.

RNDS 3, 7, AND 11: *P2, k1tbl, p2, [yo, ssk] 2 times; rep from *.

RNDS 5 AND 9: *P2, k1tbl, p2, [k2tog, yo] 2 times; rep from *.

RND 13: *P2, M1P, k1tbl, M1P, p2, [k2tog, yo] 2 times; rep from *—patt rep has inc'd to a multiple of 11 sts.

RNDS 14, 16, AND 18: *P3, k1tbl, p3, k4; rep from *.

RNDS 15 AND 19: *P3, k1tbl, p3, [yo, ssk] 2 times; rep from *.

RND 17: *P3, k1tbl, p3, [k2tog, yo] 2 times; rep from*.

RND 20: *P3, k1tbl, p3, k4; rep from *.

Repeat as given in directions.

UPPER BODICE PATTERN *(EVEN NUMBER OF STS)*

ROWS 1 AND 3: (RS) Knit.

ROW 2: (WS) P2, *yo, k2tog; rep from * to last 2 sts, p2.

ROW 4: P2, *k2tog, yo; rep from * to last 2 sts, p2.

Repeat Rows 1–4 for pattern.

Lower Body

With size 4 (3.5 mm) straight needles and using the cable method (see Glossary), CO 127 (163, 199) sts. Change to size 4 (3.5 mm) 36" (90 cm) cir needle. Do not join. To avoid twisting when joining the first lace rnd, work Rnd 1 of lower edge pattern (see Stitch Guide) as a RS row to last st, place marker (pm) on needle, and p2tog (last st tog with first st of row) to join into a rnd; the p2tog counts as the first st of Rnd 2—126 (162, 198) sts rem. Work to end of Rnd 2. Work Rnds 3 and 4 once, then rep Rnds 1–4 three more times—16 rnds total; piece measures about 2¼" (5.5 cm) from CO.

DEC RND: (counts as Rnd 1 of lacy stripe patt) With size 3 (3.25 mm) needle, *p2tog, k1tbl, p2tog, [k2tog, yo] 2 times; rep from * to end, changing to same-size 24" (60 cm) cir needle if necessary—98 (126, 154) sts; 49 (63, 77) sts each for front and back.

Work Rnds 2–4 of lacy stripe patt (see Stitch Guide), then rep Rnds 1–4 until piece measures 11¾" (30 cm) from CO, or desired length to underbust, ending with Rnd 4.

FRONT BUST SHAPING

Work 49 (63, 77) back sts in established lacy stripe patt, place marker (pm), work Rnd 1 of front bodice patt (see Stitch Guide) over 49 (63, 77) front sts and *at the same time* inc them to 63 (81, 99) sts—112 (144, 176) sts total. Work 11 rnds even, cont established lacy stripe patt on back sts, and working Rnds 2–12 of front bodice patt front sts.

NEXT RND: Work 49 (63, 77) back sts in established lacy stripe patt, work Rnd 13 of front bodice patt over 63 (81, 99) front sts and inc them to 77 (99, 121) sts, changing to same size 36" (90 cm) cir needle if necessary—126 (162, 198) sts total.

Work 14 (18, 22) rnds even, cont established lacy stripe patt on back sts, and work Rnds 14–20 of front bodice patt once, then rep Rnds 17–20 of patt 1 (2, 3) more time(s), then work Rnds 17–19 once, ending with Rnd 19 of front bodice patt and Rnd 3 of lacy stripe patt—piece measures about 15½" (16¼, 16¾)" (39.5 [41.5, 42.5] cm) from CO, or desired length to underarms (see Notes).

DIVIDE FOR FRONTS AND BACK

Work Rnd 4 of established patt across 49 (63, 77) back sts, remove side m, work next 5 sts as p3tog, k1tbl, p1, place 52 (66, 80) sts just worked on holder for back, work next 37 (48, 59) sts for left front as p2, [k4, p3, k1tbl, p3] 3 (4, 5) times, k2, join new yarn at center front, work next 35 (46, 57) sts for right front as k2, [p3, k1tbl, p2, k4] 2 (3, 4) times, p3, k1tbl, p3, [yo, k1] 2 times, p2—37 (48, 59) sts at each side.

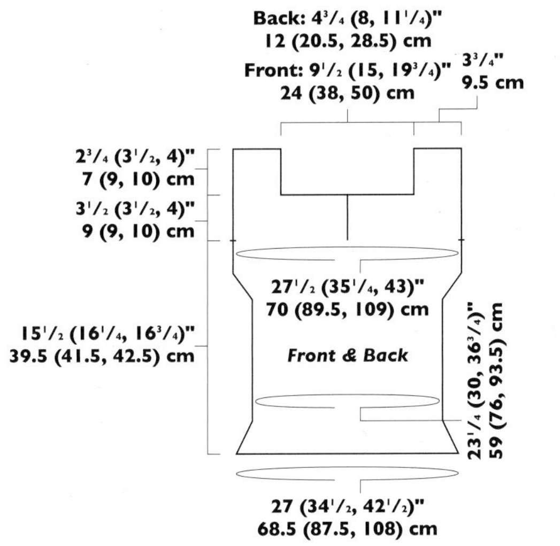

Fronts

With RS facing, join a separate ball of yarn to each group of 37 (48, 59) front sts on needle, ready to work a RS row. Work each side separately back and forth in rows as foll:

ROW 1: (RS) For left front, p2, *[k2tog, yo] 2 times, p3, k1tbl, p3; rep from * to last 2 sts, k2; for right front, k2, **p3, k1tbl, p3, [k2tog, yo] 2 times; rep from ** to last 2 sts, p2.

ROWS 2 AND 4: (WS) For right front, k2, *p4, k3, p1tbl, k3; rep from * to last 2 sts, p2; for left front, p2, **k3, p1tbl, k3, p4; rep from ** to last 2 sts, k2.

ROW 3: For left front, p2, *[yo, ssk] 2 times, p3, k1tbl, p3; rep from * to last 2 sts, k2; for right front, k2, **p3, k1tbl, p3, [yo, ssk] 2 times; rep from ** to last 2 sts, p2.

Rep the last 4 rows 2 (2, 3) more times, ending with WS Row 4—piece measures about 1¾" (1¾, 2¼)" (4.5 [4.5, 5.5] cm) from dividing rnd. Change to upper bodice patt (see Stitch Guide) and work Row 1, dec 1 (0, 1) st—36 (48, 58) sts at each side. Cont even in patt until piece measures 3½" (3½, 4)" (9 [9, 10] cm) from dividing rnd, ending with WS Row 4 of patt.

Back: 4¾ (8, 11¼)"
12 (20.5, 28.5) cm

Front: 9½ (15, 19¾)"
24 (38, 50) cm

3¾"
9.5 cm

2¾ (3½, 4)"
7 (9, 10) cm

3½ (3½, 4)"
9 (9, 10) cm

27½ (35¼, 43)"
70 (89.5, 109) cm

Front & Back

15½ (16¼, 16¾)"
39.5 (41.5, 42.5) cm

23¼ (30, 36¾)"
59 (76, 93.5) cm

27 (34½, 42½)"
68.5 (87.5, 108) cm

FRONT STRAPS

(RS) Work Row 1 of upper bodice patt over first 16 sts for left front strap, then use size 2 (2.75 mm) cir needle to BO rem 20 (32, 42) left front sts using the decrease method (see Glossary). Using the decrease method and size 2 (2.75 mm) cir needle, BO first 20 (32, 42) sts of right front—1 st rem on right needle after last BO. Transfer rem st to size 2 (2.75 mm) cir needle, and counting last BO st as first st of patt, work Row 1 of upper bodice patt over rem 15 sts for right front strap—16 sts for each strap. Working each strap separately, cont even in patt until straps measures 2¾ (3½, 4)″ (7 [9, 10] cm), ending with Row 4 of patt—piece measures about 6¼ (7, 8)″ (16 [18, 20.5] cm) from dividing rnd. Place straps on separate holders.

Back

Return 52 (66, 80) held back sts to size 2 (2.75 mm) needle and rejoin yarn with RS facing, ready to work a RS row.

ROW 1: (RS) *P1, k1tbl, p1, [k2tog, yo] 2 times; rep from * to last 3 sts, p1, k1tbl, p1.

ROWS 2 AND 4: (WS) K1, p1tbl, k1, *p4, k1, p1tbl, k1; rep from *.

ROW 3: *P1, k1tbl, p1, [yo, ssk] 2 times; rep from * to last 3 sts, p1, k1tbl, p1.

Rep the last 4 rows 2 (2, 3) more times, ending with WS Row 4—piece measures about 1¾ (1¾, 2¼)″ (4.5 [4.5, 5.5] cm) from dividing rnd. Change to upper bodice patt, and work even in patt until piece measures 3½ (3½, 4)″ (9 [9, 10] cm) from dividing rnd, ending with WS Row 4 of patt.

BACK STRAPS

(RS) Work Row 1 of upper bodice patt over first 16 sts for right back strap, join new yarn, then use size 2 (2.75 mm) cir needle to BO center 20 (34, 48) sts using the decrease method—1 st rem on right needle after last BO. Counting last BO st as first st of patt, work Row 1 of upper bodice patt over rem 15 sts for left back strap—16 sts for each strap. Working each strap separately, cont even in patt until straps measures 2¾ (3½, 4)″ (7 [9, 10] cm), ending with Row 4 of patt. Place straps on separate holders

Finishing

With CO tail threaded on a tapestry needle, neaten join in first rnd of lower body. Block to measurements.

STRAPS

Temporarily pin held sts at ends of straps tog and try on garment. Add or remove rows as necessary to adjust strap length. With yarn threaded on a tapestry needle, use the Kitchener st (see Glossary) to graft ends of straps tog at shoulder line.

NECK EDGING

With longer size 2 (2.75 mm) cir needle, RS facing, and beg right back neck, pick up and knit 21 (36, 51) sts across back neck (pick up about 9 sts for every 2″ [5 cm]), 25 (31, 36) sts along neck edge of left strap, 21 (34, 44) sts across left front neck to front opening, 16 (16, 18) sts down left edge of front opening, 16 (16, 18) sts up right edge of front opening, 21 (34, 44) sts across right front neck, and 25 (31, 36) sts along neck edge of right strap—145 (198, 247) sts total. BO all sts using the picot method as foll: BO 2 sts (1 st on right needle), *return st on right needle to left needle, use the cable method to CO 1 st, BO 3 sts; rep from * to end, fasten off last st.

ARMHOLE EDGING

With crochet hook and RS facing, join yarn to base of armhole. Work 77 (87, 99) single crochet sts (sc; see Glossary) evenly spaced around armhole, join with a sl st in first st, do not cut yarn. With shorter size 2 (2.75 mm) cir needle and RS facing, pick up and knit 1 st for each sc around—77 (87, 99) sts. Working in the rnd with RS facing, work picot BO as for neck edging. Rep for other armhole. Weave in loose ends.

BUTTONS AND BUTTON LOOPS

Sew buttons to left front, the lowest ½″ (1.3 cm) up from the bottom of front opening, the highest centered on the upper bodice patt, and the rem button centered in between. With single strand of yarn threaded on tapestry needle, make a thread loop on right front opposite each buttonhole, beg and ending each loop on WS of right front along pick-up row for neck edging so that picot BO overlaps the base of each loop.

RIBBON TIE

Beg and end at corners at top of front opening, thread ribbon through eyelets of upper bodice patt all the way around the neck opening as shown. Draw up ribbon, gathering neckline to where best fit is achieved, and tie in a bow at front.

DELPHINE

NIOBE ✳ *lacy bell-sleeve pullover*

No description of life in the French countryside would be complete without mention of the fabled noontime lunch. City dwellers also keep those delightful midday hours (albeit sometimes compressed). But for true immersion in the ritual, plant yourself along any roadside during the warmer months and observe. At the stroke of *midi*, the entire country becomes a giant picnic ground. Cars pull over, portable tables are set up in a flash, bottles of wine are uncorked, *patés* and *baguettes* appear, and the nation settles in for two to three hours of *le déjeuner*.

One of my most indelible Gallic images is of our lunch dining shoulder-to-shoulder with acres of sunflowers. It's easy to see why artists and poets were drawn to them and all things that bloom in the honeyed light of the South.

Niobe offers an almost yin counterpoint to all this golden brilliance. The enigmatic blend of yarns that suggest shade and midnight twine around each other, creating a shadowy hourglass figure that complements the bright day. A diminishing triangle of spidery lace festoons the hem and sleeves, and a demurely tantalizing glimpse of sun-warmed skin provides intrigue.

FINISHED SIZE

29½ (32¾, 36, 39¼, 42½, 45½)" (75 [83, 91.5, 99.5, 108, 115.5] cm) bust circumference. Sweater shown measures 29½" (75 cm). NOTE: This garment is designed with about 3" to 5" (7.5 to 12.5 cm) negative wearing ease for a close, body-conscious fit.

YARN

Worsted weight (#4 Medium), or two strands of sportweight (#2 Fine) used together.

SHOWN HERE: Rowan Kid Classic (70% lambswool, 26% kid mohair, 4% nylon; 153 yd [140 ml/50 g): #831 smoke (charcoal), 3 (4, 4, 4, 5, 5) balls.

Rowan Kidsilk Night (67% kid mohair, 18% silk, 10% polyester, 5% nylon; 227 yd [208 ml/25 g): #610 starry night (black), 2 (3, 3, 3, 3, 4) balls. NOTE: This yarn has been discontinued; substitute the laceweight mohair/silk yarn of your choice.

NEEDLES

BODY AND SLEEVES: size U.S. 11 (8 mm): 12", 24", and 36" (30, 60, and 90 cm) circular (cir); double-pointed needles (dpn) may be substituted for shortest cir needle. NECKBAND: size U.S. 8 (5 mm): 24" (60 cm) cir. *Adjust needle size if necessary to obtain the correct gauge.*

NOTIONS

Markers (m); removable markers; stitch holders; tapestry needle.

GAUGE

10 stitches and 16 rounds = 4" (10 cm) in stockinette stitch and lace patterns from charts with 2 strands of yarn held together on larger needles.

Notes

- The sleeves and lower body are worked separately in the round to the armholes, then joined for working the yoke circularly to the neck edge. A narrow lace panel extends from the belled sleeve cuff all the way up the center of the sleeve to the neck edge.
- Use two strands of sportweight (#2 Fine) yarn throughout.
- A single strand of worsted-weight (#4 Medium) yarn may be substituted for two strands of sportweight yarn, if desired. Be sure to get the correct gauge using the new yarn, aiming for a slightly more open, stretchy fabric than is typical for worsted yarn at its usual gauge.

Sleeve (make 2)

With shortest cir needle or dpn in larger size and both yarns tog, CO 38 sts. Do not join. To avoid twisting when joining the first lace rnd, work Rnd 1 of Sleeve chart as a RS row to last st, place marker (pm) on needle, k2tog (last st tog with first st of row) to join into a rnd; the k2tog counts as the first st of Rnd 2—37 sts rem. Knit to end of Rnd 2, then work Rnds 3–54 of chart—29 sts; piece measures about 13½" (34.5 cm) from CO. From here until the end of the sleeve, work center 5 sts in marked lace patt shown on Rnds 47–54 of chart, and work all other sts in St st. *At the same time* work inc rnd on next rnd after chart as foll: K1, M1 (see Glossary), knit to last st, M1, k1—2 sts inc'd. Work 5 (4, 3, 3, 3, 2) rnds even in patt. Cont in patt, rep the shaping of the last 6 (5, 4, 4, 4, 3) rnds 3 (3, 5, 4, 1, 8) more time(s)—37 (37, 41, 39, 33, 47) sts. Work inc rnd on next 0 (1, 0, 1, 1, 0) rnd, then work 0 (3, 0, 2, 2, 0) rnds even, then rep the shaping of the last 0 (4, 0, 3, 3, 0) rnds 0 (0, 0, 1, 5, 0) more time(s)—37 (39, 41, 43, 45, 47) sts; piece measures about 19½ (19½, 19½, 20, 20, 20¼)" (49.5 [49.5, 49.5, 51, 51, 51.5] cm) from CO. Note the last patt rnd completed on center lace panel so you can resume the patt with the correct rnd later when working the yoke. Place 4 (4, 5, 5, 6, 6) sts at each end of rnd on holder for underarm for 8 (8, 10, 10, 12, 12) underarm sts total, then place rem 29 (31, 31, 33, 33, 35) sts on separate holder.

Lower Body

With middle-length cir needle in larger size and both yarns held tog, CO 87 (95, 103, 111, 119, 127) sts. Do not join. Work Rnd 1 of Body chart as a RS row to establish patts and join as foll: *K3 (5, 7, 9, 11, 13), place marker (pm), work 37 sts of Rnd 1, pm, k3 (5, 7, 9, 11, 13),* pm for side "seam"; rep from * to * to last st, pm for end-of-rnd, k2tog (last st tog with first st of row) to join into a rnd; the k2tog counts as the first st of Rnd 2—86 (94, 102, 110, 118, 126) sts rem; 43 (47, 51, 55, 59, 63) sts each for back and front. Knit to end of Rnd 2. Keeping outside marked lace sections in St st, work Rnds 3–32 of chart—54 (62, 70, 78, 86, 94) sts after completing Rnd 32; 27 (31, 35, 39, 43, 47) sts each for front and back; piece measures about 8" (20.5 cm) from CO.

Sleeve

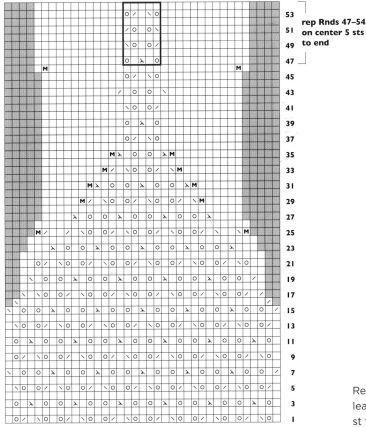

rep Rnds 47–54
on center 5 sts
to end

Row numbers: 53, 51, 49, 47, 45, 43, 41, 39, 37, 35, 33, 31, 29, 27, 25, 23, 21, 19, 17, 15, 13, 11, 9, 7, 5, 3, 1

Body

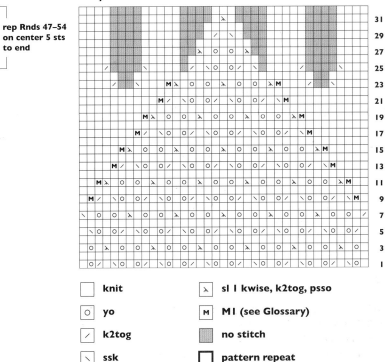

Row numbers: 31, 29, 27, 25, 23, 21, 19, 17, 15, 13, 11, 9, 7, 5, 3, 1

☐ knit	⅄	sl 1 kwise, k2tog, psso
○ yo	M	M1 (see Glossary)
╱ k2tog	▨	no stitch
╲ ssk	☐	pattern repeat

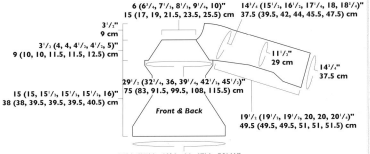

6 (6³/₄, 7¹/₂, 8¹/₄, 9¹/₄, 10)"
15 (17, 19, 21.5, 23.5, 25.5) cm

14³/₄ (15¹/₂, 16¹/₄, 17¹/₄, 18, 18³/₄)"
37.5 (39.5, 42, 44, 45.5, 47.5) cm

3¹/₂"
9 cm

3¹/₂ (4, 4, 4¹/₂, 4¹/₂, 5)"
9 (10, 10, 11.5, 11.5, 12.5) cm

11¹/₂"
29 cm

14³/₄"
37.5 cm

29¹/₂ (32³/₄, 36, 39¹/₄, 42¹/₂, 45¹/₂)"
75 (83, 91.5, 99.5, 108, 115.5) cm

15 (15, 15¹/₂, 15¹/₂, 15¹/₂, 16)"
38 (38, 39.5, 39.5, 39.5, 40.5) cm

Front & Back

19¹/₂ (19¹/₂, 19¹/₂, 20, 20, 20¹/₄)"
49.5 (49.5, 49.5, 51, 51, 51.5) cm

34¹/₂ (37¹/₂, 40³/₄, 44, 47¹/₄, 50¹/₂)"
87.5 (95, 103.5, 112, 120, 128.5) cm

Remove m on each side of lace section as you come to them, leaving side "seam" and end-of-rnd m in place. Work even in St st for 16 rnds—piece measures about 12″ (30.5 cm) from CO.

NEXT RND: *Knit to 6 sts before side m, M1, k1, M1, k5 to m, sl m, k5, M1, k1, M1; rep from * once more, knit to end—62 (70, 78, 86, 94, 102) sts.

Knit 1 rnd.

NEXT RND: *Knit to 1 st before side m, M1, k1, sl m, k1, M1; rep from * once more, knit to end—4 sts inc'd.

Knit 1 rnd. Rep the shaping of the last 2 rnds 2 more times—74 (82, 90, 98, 106, 114) sts. Work 4 (4, 6, 6, 6, 8) rnds even in St st—piece measures about 15 (15, 15¹/₂, 15¹/₂, 15¹/₂, 16)″ (38 [38, 39.5, 39.5, 39.5, 40.5] cm) from CO. Place 4 (4, 5, 5, 6, 6) sts each side of each m on separate holders for underarms for 8 (8, 10, 10, 12, 12) sts on each holder, then place one group of 29 (33, 35, 39, 41, 45) sts on separate holder for front—29 (33, 35, 39, 41, 45) back sts rem.

Yoke

Rejoin yarn to beg of back sts with RS facing.

RND 1: Using longest cir needle in largest size, k29 (33, 35, 39, 41, 45) back sts, pm, work 29 (31, 31, 33, 33, 35) held left sleeve sts in established patts, pm, k29 (33, 35, 39, 41, 45) held front sts, pm, work 29 (31, 31, 33, 33, 35) held right sleeve sts in established patts, pm, and join for working in rnds—116 (128, 132, 144, 148, 160) sts total.

RND 2: *Knit to last 2 back sts, k3tog removing m and hanging a removable marker in the new dec st (*not* on the needle between sts), work in patt to last st of left sleeve, k3togtbl (see Glossary) removing m and hanging removable m in new dec st, knit to last 2 sts of front, k3tog removing m and hanging removable m in new dec st, work in patt to last st of right sleeve, k3togtbl (last st of right sleeve tog with first 2 sts of back) removing end-of-rnd m and hanging removable m in new dec st—108 (120, 124, 136, 140, 152) sts; 4 marked raglan sts; 25 (29, 31, 35, 37, 41) sts each for back and front; 27 (29, 29, 31, 31, 33) sts each sleeve.

RNDS 3–5: Knit.

RND 6: Ssk, *work in patt to 2 sts before marked st, k2tog, knit marked st, ssk; rep from * 2 more times, work in patt to 2 sts before last marked st, k2tog, knit marked st—8 sts dec'd; 2 sts dec'd each from back, front, and each sleeve.

RND 7: Knit.

Rep the last 2 rnds 2 (3, 3, 4, 4, 5) more times, changing to medium-length cir needle in larger size when necessary—84 (88, 92, 96, 100, 104) sts; 4 marked raglan sts; 19 (21, 23, 25, 27, 29) sts each for back and front; 21 sts for each sleeve for all sizes. Change to smaller cir needle.

NEXT RND: *[P1, k1] 9 (10, 11, 12, 13, 14) times, p1, knit marked st, [p1, k1] 10 times, p1, knit marked st; rep from * once more.

NEXT RND: Work k2togtbl or p2togtbl as needed to maintain patt, *work in established rib patt to 2 sts before marked st, work k2tog or p2tog as needed, knit marked st, work k2togtbl or p2togtbl as needed; rep from * 2 more times, work in patt to 2 sts before last marked st, work k2tog or p2tog as needed, knit marked st—8 sts dec'd; 2 sts dec'd each from back, front, and each sleeve.

Work 1 rnd even, working all sts as they appear (knit the knits and purl the purls). Rep the last 2 rnds 1 more time—68 (72, 76, 80, 84, 88) sts; 4 marked raglan sts; 15 (17, 19, 21, 23, 25) sts each for back and front; 17 sts for each sleeve; yoke measures about 3½ (4, 4, 4½, 4½, 5)" (9 [10, 10, 11.5, 11.5, 12.5] cm) from joining rnd. BO all sts in rib patt.

Finishing

With yarn threaded on a tapestry needle, use the Kitchener st (see Glossary) to graft held sleeve and body sts together at underarms. Weave in loose ends. Block to measurements, coaxing sleeve sections at top of yoke upward in a gentle curve to form a scooped neckline as shown on schematic.

NIOBE

BOTTOM-UP SEAMLESS RAGLAN CONSTRUCTION

Considering that many patterns specify working a garment in pieces from the hem to the neckline, most knitters learn to construct garments that way. This method can make custom fitting difficult because it isn't clear how the pieces fit together until all of the knitting is completed and the seams are sewn. Anyone's enthusiasm can wane, when, after hours of seaming, there's the nasty shock of an ill-fitting garment. Seamless bottom-up construction, on the other hand, lets you try on the garment as it progresses as well as cast on lovely scalloped lace edgings at the hem and sleeves. The sweaters that follow this type of construction are Stella (page 56) and Niobe (page 84). Satine (page 10) and Delphine (page 78) are worked in modifications of this technique.

You construct bottom-up seamless garments in the same way as their made-in-pieces sisters, but you knit the front and back simultaneously in a single piece to the armholes, work the sleeves in rounds from the cuffs to the underarms, then join the pieces and work the yoke in a single piece to the neck. Elizabeth Zimmermann and Jacqueline Fee both provide excellent tutorials for bottom-up seamless raglans (see the Bibliography, page 157). Their methods are perfect for a roomy sweater with a relaxed fit, but for the garments in this book, I've made modifications to achieve hourglass shaping and a closer fit in the upper body.

For a pullover, cast on stitches for the entire lower circumference, using a circular needle at least 40" (101.5 cm) long, or two shorter circular needles. Join the stitches and work in rounds until the piece measures the desired length to the underarm (usually just after reaching the fullest part of the bust). Shape the waist along the way as desired (Figure 1). (For more information about shaping the waist, see Knit to Fit on page 53.) Place a few stitches on holders at each underarm, then set this piece aside. Work each sleeve separately in rounds from the cuff to the underarm, then place the same number of stitches on holders at each sleeve underarm (Figure 2).

To join the body and sleeves onto the same long circular needle with the round beginning at the left back shoulder, knit the left sleeve stitches, place a marker, knit across the front stitches, place another marker, knit across the right sleeve stitches, place a marker, then knit across the back stitches and place a final marker (Figure 3). Decreases are worked at specific intervals along the four marked raglan lines to decrease stitches equally on the front, back, and sleeves to the neck (Figure 4). You approach a cardigan much the same way, but you work the body and yoke back and forth in rows, beginning and ending at the center front.

To reduce the amount of fabric in the upper body, I like to work a round or two plain, then work decreases every round for about 2" to 3" (5 to 7.5 cm). On some of the modifications in this book, I work the decreases spaced evenly around the full circumference as for circular yoke construction. This approach allows for more rapid decreasing than just along the four raglan lines. I also add short-rows to some of the sleeve caps and center backs to finesse the shape of the yoke.

TIPS FOR BOTTOM-UP RAGLAN CONSTRUCTION

- Be sure to work your gauge swatch in the round. Many knitters have tighter or looser tension when they work in rounds than when they work back and forth in rows.

- Work the sleeves first to learn the stitch pattern and verify your gauge before you cast on for the entire lower body circumference. (This approach is my favorite aspect of this construction type.)

- If you have sloped or narrow shoulders, as you work the yoke, you may need to add more short-rows in the back than the pattern calls for. Your body is your best guide.

- To ensure the proper fit, measure a sweater you already own that fits you well and use the measurements to help fit this garment. Also, try on your work as you go. It's easy to adjust for sleeve and body length along the way.

- For an in-depth discussion of converting existing patterns from flat to seamless knitting, refer to Barbara Walker's *Second Treasury of Knitting Patterns*.

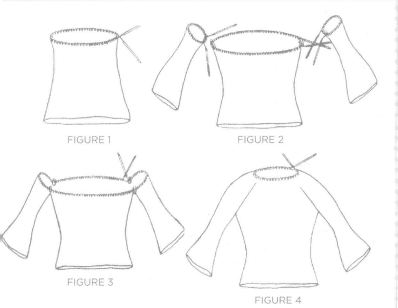

FIGURE 1

FIGURE 2

FIGURE 3

FIGURE 4

CELESTE ✳ *mohair lingerie wrap*

FINISHED SIZE

34 (38, 42, 45, 49)" (86.5 [96.5, 106.5, 114.5, 124.5] cm) bust circumference. Sweater shown measures 34" (86.5 cm).

YARN

Sportweight (#2 Fine).

SHOWN HERE: Rowan Kidsilk Haze (70% kid mohair, 30% silk; 227 yd [208 ml/25 g]): #634 cream, 6 (7, 7, 8, 9) balls.

NEEDLES

BODY, SLEEVES, AND NECKBAND: size U.S. 8 (5 mm) one 16" (40 cm) and two 36" (90 cm) circular (cir), and set of 4 or 5 double-pointed (dpn). CUFFS, SLEEVES, FRONT BANDS, AND PROVISIONAL CAST-ON: size U.S. 7 (4.5 mm): straight. *Adjust needle size if necessary to obtain the correct gauge.*

NOTIONS

Markers (m); stitch holders; removable markers or waste yarn; smooth cotton waste yarn for provisional cast-on; size G/6 (4.25 mm) crochet hook; tapestry needle.

GAUGE

19 stitches and 27 rows/rounds = 4" (10 cm) in slip-stitch pattern on larger needles; 19 stitches and 25 rows = 4" (10 cm) in St st on larger needles; 21 stitches and 32 rows (1 repeat wide and 2 repeats high) of diamond pattern from chart measure 4" (10 cm) wide and 5" (12.5 cm) high on smaller needles, after blocking.

*E*urope, and especially France, has long drawn American artists and musicians to its shores, from the flamboyant Josephine Baker to my own mother, Yvonne. At sixty-plus, *maman* made a swing through the smoky jazz clubs of the Continent with my percussionist brother as one of her side-men. She always had a fancy for beautiful clothes, but she was also a Depression-era baby with an extremely frugal side, so my sisters and I often whipped up slinky outfits for her gigs; her well-remembered "caftan phase" had us stitching together mountains of shimmering polyester.

She would have loved Celeste, though I'd be knitting it for her. The finer domestic skills eluded my mother, or she eluded them. Two things consumed her: our family of eight and her music. A comment we still hear when her name comes up is "That woman could sing!"

Notes

This garment is worked in two halves. Each half begins with a lace cuff worked in two pieces that are grafted together so the lace pattern is oriented the same way up on the front and back of each sleeve.

Stitches are picked up along one selvedge of the completed cuff and worked in the round to the top of the sleeve with shaping to create a belled shape.

Stitches are cast on at each side of the sleeve for the back and front using a provisional method, then work continues back and forth in rows to the neck edge, with a short-rowed gore at the lower edge the back. After the front stitches have been placed on a holder, the back stitches are worked separately to the center back where a third gore is worked on the left half only. The completed halves of the body are grafted together at the center back.

The lace front band is worked in two pieces that are grafted together at the back neck so the lace pattern is oriented right side up on both sides of the front opening.

When working short-rows for gores and neckband, slip any edge stitches at the beginning of right-side (RS) rows as if to purl with yarn in back, and slip any edge stitches at the beginning of wrong-side (WS) rows as if to purl with yarn in front.

The center back gusset is shown on the schematic as part of the left half; it is not worked on the right half. The schematic does not show the lower edging which adds about 1" (2.5 cm) to the length of the lower body after finishing.

Stitch Guide

TWISTED DOUBLE DECREASE

Sl 2 sts as if to k2tog through their back loops, k1, pass 2 slipped sts over—2 sts dec'd.

KRB

Knit into st in the row below the next st on left needle—1 st inc'd.

SLIP-STITCH PATTERN IN ROUNDS *(EVEN NUMBER OF STS)*

RNDS 1–4: Knit.

RND 5: *P1, sl 1 as if to purl with yarn in front (pwise wyf); rep from *.

RND 6: *K1, sl 1 pwise wyf; rep from *.

Repeat Rnds 1–6 for pattern.

SLIP-STITCH PATTERN IN ROWS *(EVEN NUMBER OF STS)*

ROWS 1 AND 3: (RS) Sl 1 pwise with yarn back (wyb), knit to end.

ROWS 2 AND 4: (WS) Sl 1 pwise wyf, purl to end.

ROW 5: Sl 1 pwise wyb, *p1, sl 1 pwise wyf; rep from * to last st, k1.

ROW 6: Sl 1 pwise wyf, p2, *sl 1 pwise wyb, p1; rep from * to last st, p1.

Repeat Rows 1–6 for pattern.

Diamond

[Diamond chart — rows 1–15 (odd-numbered rows labeled: 1, 3, 5, 7, 9, 11, 13, 15)]

Legend

☐ k on RS; p on WS	⟍	ssk
☐ · p on RS; k on WS	λ	twisted double dec (see Stitch Guide)
☐ o yo	☑ V	sl 1 (see Notes)
☐ ⁄ k2tog		

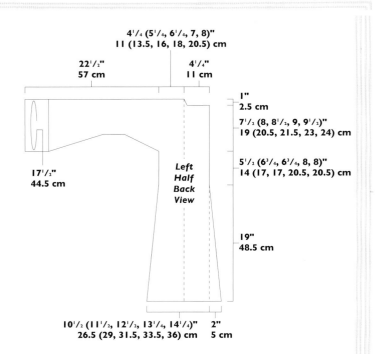

4¼ (5¼, 6¼, 7, 8)"
11 (13.5, 16, 18, 20.5) cm

22½"
57 cm

4¼"
11 cm

1"
2.5 cm

7½ (8, 8½, 9, 9½)"
19 (20.5, 21.5, 23, 24) cm

5½ (6¾, 6¾, 8, 8)"
14 (17, 17, 20.5, 20.5) cm

17½"
44.5 cm

Left
Half
Back
View

19"
48.5 cm

10½ (11½, 12½, 13¼, 14¼)"
26.5 (29, 31.5, 33.5, 36) cm

2"
5 cm

Left Half

CUFF

With smaller straight needles, crochet hook, and smooth waste yarn, use the crochet-on method (see Glossary) to provisionally CO 21 sts. Change to main yarn and work Rows 1–16 of Diamond chart 3 times, then work Rows 1–8 once more—56 rows completed. Place sts on holder. Carefully remove waste yarn from provisional CO and place 21 exposed sts on straight needles. Mark each end of these sts with waste yarn or removable markers to indicate underarm side of cuff. Rejoin yarn with RS facing and work Rows 1–16 of Lace chart 3 times, then work Rows 1–8 once more—56 rows this half of cuff; 112 patt rows total. Place sts on holder. Block lightly to 17½" (44.5 cm) long and 4" (10 cm) wide. With yarn threaded on a tapestry needle and RS facing, use the Kitchener st (see Glossary) to graft the live sts at each end of cuff tog.

SLEEVE

Hold cuff horizontally with marked underarm join on the right. With RS facing, 16" (40 cm) cir needle in larger size, and beg at marked underarm of cuff, pick up and knit 40 sts along cuff selvedge to grafted centerline for left back sleeve (about 3 sts for every 2 slipped cuff edge sts), then 40 sts along cuff selvedge from centerline to underarm for left front sleeve—80 sts total. Place marker (pm) and join for working in rnds. Work Rnds 1–6 of slip-stitch patt in rnds (see Stitch Guide) 0 (1, 1, 1, 0) time(s), then work Rnds 1–3 of patt.

SLEEVE DEC RND: (Rnd 4 of patt) K2tog, knit to last 2 sts, ssk—2 sts dec'd.

Work Rnds 5 and 6 of patt. Rep Rnds 1–6 of patt 11 (10, 10, 9, 9) more times, working sleeve dec rnd on Rnd 4 of each rep and changing to dpn in larger size if there are too few sts to fit around cir needle—56 (58, 58, 60, 60) sts rem; piece measures about 14½ (14½, 14½, 13¾, 13)" (37 [37, 37, 35, 33] cm) from lower edge of cuff. Work even in patt for 18 (12, 6, 6, 6) rnds, ending with Rnd 6 for all sizes.

SLEEVE INC RND: (Rnd 1 of patt) K1, krb (see Stitch Guide), work in patt to last st, krb, k1—2 sts inc'd.

Work Rnds 2 and 3 even in patt, rep the sleeve inc rnd on Rnd 4 of patt, then work Rnds 5 and 6 of patt—2 sts inc'd. Cont in patt, rep the shaping of the last 6 rnds 5 (6, 7, 8, 9) more times, working the sleeve inc rnd on Rnds 1 and 4 of each rep and changing back to 16" (40 cm) cir needle in larger size when there are too many sts to fit around dpn—80 (86, 90, 96, 100) sts; piece measures about 22½″ (57 cm) from lower edge of cuff for all sizes. Place a removable marker in the center of the last sleeve rnd completed to indicate end of sleeve at shoulder line.

FRONT AND BACK

With crochet hook, smooth waste yarn, and using the crochet-on method, CO 117 (123, 123, 129, 129) sts for left back onto smaller needle. Join new yarn to beg of CO sts with RS facing. With 36″ (90 cm) cir needle in larger size, knit to last new CO st, work next 2 sts (last CO st and first sleeve st) tog as k2tog, knit to last sleeve st, set aside temporarily. With straight needle and working from lower edge to underarm, pick up 117 (123, 123, 129, 129) sts for left front from main yarn loops at base of provisional CO sts. With RS facing and yarn attached to end of sleeve, work next 2 sts (last sleeve st and first CO st) tog as ssk, knit to end—312 (330, 334, 352, 356) sts total; row just completed counts as Row 1 of slip-stitch patt in rows (see Stitch Guide). NOTE: Because there are sts worked from both sides of the same provisional CO, the cable section of the cir needle will be folded in half in a tight hairpin bend; it will become easier to slide the sts around this bend as the work progresses. Work Rows 2–6 of patt once, then rep Rows 1–6 of patt 3 more times, ending with a WS row.

Left Back Gore

Work short-rows to shape gore at lower left back as foll:

SHORT-ROW 1: (RS) Sl 1 (see Notes), k89, turn.

SHORT-ROWS 2, 4, 6, 8, 10, AND 12: (RS) Yo, purl to end, turn.

SHORT-ROW 3: Sl 1, k87, turn.

SHORT-ROW 5: Sl 1, k85, turn.

SHORT-ROW 7: Sl 1, k83, turn.

SHORT-ROW 9: Sl 1, k81, turn.

SHORT-ROW 11: Sl 1, k79, turn.

SHORT-ROW 13: (RS, counts as Row 1 of patt) Sl 1, [knit to yo, work yo tog with st after it as k2tog] 6 times, knit to end.

Work Rows 2–6 of patt across all sts, then rep Rows 1–6 of patt 0 (1, 2, 3, 4) more time(s)—piece measures about 4¼ (5¼, 6¼, 7, 8)″ (11 [13.5, 16, 18, 20.5] cm) from end of sleeve at shoulder line and 6¼ (7¼, 8¼, 9, 10)″ (16 [18.5, 21, 23, 25.5] cm) from front and back CO at back edge (beg of RS rows).

Left Back

(RS, Row 1 of patt) Work 156 (165, 167, 176, 178) back sts, place rem 156 (165, 167, 176, 178) sts on holder for left front; held sts

of left front edge are shown as dotted line on schematic. Work Rows 2–6 of patt and *at the same time* BO 2 (3, 3, 2, 2) sts at beg of WS Row 2, then BO 2 sts at beg of WS Row 4—152 (160, 162, 172, 174) sts rem. Work 14 rows even in St st, ending with a WS row, then work Rows 1–6 of patt once more.

Center Back Gore

Work Short-rows 1–13 as for left back gore, ending with RS Short-row 13 (counts as RS Row 1 of patt), then work WS Row 2 of patt across all sts—piece measures about 4¼" (11 cm) for all sizes from where front sts were put on hold at shoulder line, 8½ (9½, 10½, 11¼, 12¼)" (21.5 [24, 26.5, 28.5, 31] cm) from end of sleeve at shoulder line and from front and back CO at bustline, and 12½ (13½, 14½, 15¼, 16¼)" (31.5 [34.5, 37, 38.5, 41.5] cm) from front and back CO at lower back edge (beg of RS rows). Place sts on holder.

Right Half

CUFF AND SLEEVE

Work as for left half—80 (86, 90, 96, 100) sts; piece measures about 22½" (57 cm) from lower edge of cuff for all sizes. Place a removable marker in the center of the last sleeve rnd completed to indicate end of sleeve at shoulder line.

FRONT AND BACK

With crochet hook, smooth waste yarn, and using the crochet-on method, CO 117 (123, 123, 129, 129) sts for right front onto smaller needle. Join new yarn to beg of CO sts with RS facing. With 36" (90 cm) cir needle in larger size, knit to last new CO st, work next 2 sts (last CO st and first sleeve st) tog as k2tog, knit to last sleeve st, set aside temporarily. With straight needle and working from lower edge to underarm, pick up 117 (123, 123, 129, 129) sts for right back from main yarn loops at base of provisional CO sts. With RS facing and yarn attached to end of sleeve, work next 2 sts (last sleeve st and first CO st) tog as ssk, knit to end—312 (330, 334, 352, 356) sts total; row just completed counts as Row 1 of slip-stitch patt in rows. Work Rows 2–6 of patt once, rep Rows 1–6 of patt 3 more times, then work Row 1 once more to end with a RS row.

Right Back Gore

Work short-rows to shape gore at lower right back as foll:

SHORT-ROW 1: (WS) Sl 1 (see Notes), p89, turn.

SHORT-ROWS 2, 4, 6, 8, 10, AND 12: (RS) Yo, knit to end, turn.

SHORT-ROW 3: Sl 1, p87, turn.

SHORT-ROW 5: Sl 1, p85, turn.

SHORT-ROW 7: Sl 1, p83, turn.

SHORT-ROW 9: Sl 1, p81, turn.

SHORT-ROW 11: Sl 1, p79, turn.

SHORT-ROW 13: (WS, counts as Row 2 of patt) Sl 1, [purl to yo, work yo tog with st after it as ssp (see Glossary)] 6 times, purl to end.

GRAFTING MOHAIR YARN

Mohair yarn in all its gossamer glory can be challenging to graft successfully, especially when working at large gauges and over a large number of stitches, such as with Celeste. If you have not grafted with mohair yarn before, take the time to practice with two sample swatches knitted to the same stockinette gauge as the finished garment. Use a good quality metal needle with a large eye and bent tip (I prefer Chibi brand), which will allow you to easily insert the needle tip into the stitches to be joined.

When worked at a loose gauge, mohair stitches tend to spread laterally so the stitches become very wide and short. Spread the two pieces to be joined on a flat surface where you can easily see the live stitches and graft the first 10 stitches of each piece together. Use the tip of the needle to adjust the tension along the join to match the surrounding fabric, then graft the next 10 stitches.

Because mohair yarn tends to cling to itself and not slide through the stitches easily, it is better to work using short lengths of yarn and adjust each section as you go along, rather than try to graft all at once with a single strand. Splice the lengths of grafting yarn together to avoid having knots or ends to weave in. Give yourself enough time to do this carefully and correctly, and the happy result will be an almost invisible join!

Work Rows 3–6 of patt across all sts, rep Rows 1–6 of patt 0 (1, 2, 3, 4) time(s), then work Row 1 once more—piece measures about 4¼ (5¼, 6¼, 7, 8)" (11 [13.5, 16, 18, 20.5] cm) from end of sleeve at shoulder line and 6¼ (7¼, 8¼, 9, 10)" (16 [18.5, 21, 23, 25.5] cm) from front and back CO at back edge (end of RS rows).

Right Back

(WS, Row 2 of patt) Work 156 (165, 167, 176, 178) back sts, place rem 156 (165, 167, 176, 178) sts on holder for right front. Work Rows 3–6 of patt and *at the same time* BO 2 (3, 3, 2, 2) sts at beg of RS Row 3, then BO 2 sts at beg of RS Row 5—152 (160, 162, 172, 174) sts. Work 14 rows even in St st, ending with a WS row, work Rows 1–6 of patt once, then work Rows 1 and 2 once more—piece measures about 4¼" (11 cm) for all sizes from where front sts were put on hold at shoulder line, 8½ (9½, 10½, 11¼, 12¼)" (21.5 [24, 26.5, 28.5, 31] cm) from end of sleeve at shoulder line and from front and back CO at bustline, and 10½ (11½, 12½, 13¼, 14¼)" (26.5 [29, 31.5, 33.5, 36] cm) from front and back CO at lower back edge (end of RS rows). Place sts on holder.

Finishing

Wet-block to finished measurements; right half will not include center back gusset indicated by dotted line on schematic for left half. With yarn threaded on a tapestry needle, use the Kitchener st to graft 152 (160, 162, 172, 174) held sts of the right and left backs tog. With RS facing, join yarn to beg of straight selvedge of back neck at right side and use crochet hook to stabilize back neck by working 24 single crochet sts (see Glossary) across straight selvedge edge of back neck, ending at left side. Fasten off last st.

FRONT BAND

With smaller straight needles, crochet hook, and smooth waste yarn, use the crochet-on method to CO 21 sts. Change to main yarn and work Rows 1–16 of Diamond chart 13 (14, 14, 15, 15) times, then work Rows 1–15 once more—223 (239, 239, 255, 255) rows completed. Place sts on holder. Work a second piece the same as the first. With yarn threaded on a tapestry needle and RS facing, use the Kitchener st to graft the live sts at ends of front band pieces tog.

NECKBAND EDGING

Return 156 (165, 167, 176, 178) held right front sts to 36" (90 cm) cir needle in larger size. Rejoin yarn with RS facing to the end of these sts, pm, pick up and knit 4 sts along right back neck shaping, 24 sts from crocheted back neck reinforcement, 4 sts along left back neck shaping, pm, then knit across 156 (165, 167, 176, 178) held left front sts—344 (362, 366, 384, 388) sts total. Purl 1 WS row (counts as Row 2 of patt). Shape neck edges using short-rows as foll:

SHORT-ROW 1: (RS) Work Row 3 of slip-stitch patt in rows over 144 (152, 154, 164, 166) sts, turn.

SHORT-ROW 2: (WS) Yo, work Row 4 of patt to end.

SHORT-ROW 3: Work Row 5 of patt over 142 (150, 152, 162, 164) sts, turn.

SHORT-ROW 4: Yo, work Row 6 of patt to end.

SHORT-ROW 5: Work Row 1 of patt over 140 (148 150, 160, 162) sts, turn.

SHORT-ROW 6: Work Row 2 of patt to end.

SHORT-ROW 7: (RS; counts as Row 3 of patt on both right and left fronts) [Knit to yo, work yo tog with st after it as k2tog] 3 times, knit to end.

SHORT-ROW 8: (WS) Work Row 4 of patt over 144 (152, 154, 164, 166) sts, turn.

SHORT-ROW 9: Yo, work Row 5 of patt to end.

SHORT-ROW 10: Work Row 6 of patt over 142 (150, 152, 162, 164) sts, turn.

SHORT-ROW 11: Yo, work Row 1 of patt to end.

SHORT-ROW 12: Work Row 2 of patt over 140 (148, 150, 160, 162) sts, turn.

SHORT-ROW 13: Work Row 3 of patt to end.

SHORT-ROW 14: (RS; counts as Row 4 of patt on both right and left fronts) [Purl to yo, work yo tog with st after it as ssp] 3 times, purl to end.

Knit 1 RS row, dec 8 (2, 6, 0, 4) sts evenly spaced—336 (360, 360, 384, 384) sts. Leave sts on needle.

JOIN FRONT BAND AND NECKBAND

With second 36" (90 cm) cir needle in larger size and RS facing, pick up and knit 336 (360, 360, 384, 384) sts along one selvedge of assembled front band (about 3 sts for every 2 slipped edge sts). With yarn threaded on a tapestry needle, use the Kitchener st to graft picked-up sts of front band to live neckband sts.

LOWER EDGING

Carefully remove waste yarn from provisional CO at bottom of left front band and place these 21 exposed sts on 36" (90 cm) cir needle in larger size. Join yarn with RS facing to beg of sts, knit across 21 left front band sts, pick up and knit 22 (27, 32, 36, 41) sts along left front edge to left side "seam," 58 (63, 68, 72, 77) sts from side to middle of center back gusset, 58 (63, 68, 72, 77) sts from middle of gusset to right side, 22 (27, 32, 36, 41) sts along right front to band, then carefully remove waste yarn from 21 provisional CO sts at bottom of right front band and knit across these sts—202 (222, 242, 258, 278) sts total. Knit 3 rows, beg and ending with a WS row.

NEXT ROW: (RS) *K2tog, yo; rep from * to last 2 sts, k2.

BO all sts loosely on next row. Wet-block front bands and lower edging. Weave in loose ends.

SIMONE * *flared-sleeve cowl*

FINISHED SIZE

32½ (36, 40½, 44, 48½)" (82.5 [91.5, 103, 112, 123] cm) bust circumference. Sweater shown measures 32½" (82.5 cm).

YARN

Worsted weight (#4 Medium).

SHOWN HERE: Elsebeth Lavold Baby Llama (100% baby llama; 109 yd [100 ml/50 g]): #02 linen, 11 (12, 13, 14, 15) balls.

NEEDLES

COWL AND CUFFS: sizes U.S. 10, 9, and 8 (6, 5.5, and 5 mm): 16" and 24" (40 and 60 cm) circular (cir). BODY, SLEEVES, AND BASE OF COWL: size U.S. 7 (4.5 mm): 16" and 36" (40 and 90 cm) cir. *Adjust needle size if necessary to obtain the correct gauge.*

NOTIONS

Marker (m); stitch holders or waste yarn for holders; smooth contrasting waste yarn for provisional CO; size G/6 (4.25 mm) crochet hook (if using a crocheted method for provisional cast-on, optional); tapestry needle.

GAUGE

18 stitches and 24 row/rounds = 4" (10 cm) in stockinette stitch on size 7 (4.5 mm) needles.

The scene is Paris in 1929, and two young students meet at the Sorbonne. Matched in intellect and vision, Simone de Beauvoir and Jean-Paul Sartre begin their tumultuous lifelong *histoire* together, navigating shared lovers and equally provocative shared and disparate thought, to become the parents of French existentialism.

I struggled with Sartre's work, but de Beauvoir's writings, although equally heady, gave me much I could relate to. I distinctly remember the furor when *The Second Sex* swept through my university like wildfire. The book was all we talked about for weeks, and it propelled many of us into a revolution that was long overdue.

It would be easy to imagine Simone de Beauvoir curled up in this namesake garment, tucked away at *Les Deux Magots*, typewriter at the ready, with Sartre not far removed. A snuggle-worthy cowl and flaring sleeves provide a poetic edge, while the baby camel yarn makes knitting this top-down raglan a sensual pleasure.

Note

The cowl and upper body are worked in the round in one piece from the top edge of the cowl down to the underarms. The front and back are worked in the round in one piece to where they divide for the side inserts, then are worked separately back and forth in rows. The side inserts are worked using short-rows, then the lower edging ribbing is worked in the round across the stitches of the front and back, and stitches picked up from the selvedges of the inserts. The sleeves are worked in the round from the underarms to the lower edge of the cuffs.

Stitch Guide

DOUBLE EYELET RIB *(MULTIPLE OF 4 STS)*

RND 1: *K2, yo, p2tog; rep from *.

RND 2: *K2, p2; rep from *.

Repeat Rnds 1 and 2 for pattern.

SINGLE EYELET RIB *(MULTIPLE OF 3 STS)*

RND 1: *K1, yo, p2tog; rep from *.

RND 2: *K1, p2; rep from *.

Repeat Rnds 1 and 2 for pattern.

Cowl

With size 10 (6 mm) 24" (60 cm) cir needle and using the cable method (see Glossary), CO 176 sts. Place marker (pm) and join for working in rnds, being careful not to twist sts. Work Rnds 1 and 2 of double eyelet rib (see Stitch Guide) 9 times.

NEXT RND: *K2tog, yo, p2tog; rep from *—132 sts.

Change to size 9 (5.5 mm) 24" (60 cm) needle.

NEXT RND: *K1, p2; rep from *.

Work Rnds 1 and 2 of single eyelet rib (see Stitch Guide) 7 times. Change to size 8 (5 mm) 24" (60 cm) needle and work in k1, p2 rib as established for 3 rnds.

NEXT RND: Change to size 8 (5 mm) 16" (40 cm) needle, *k1, p2tog; rep from *—88 sts rem.

Change to size 7 (4.5 mm) 16″ (60 cm) needle and work in k1, p1 rib as established for 11 rnds—piece measures about 9″ (23 cm) from CO.

Upper Body

NOTE: The RS of the body corresponds to the WS of the cowl, and the upper body is worked with the WS of the cowl facing outward so the RS of the cowl will show when the cowl is folded down. Push the cowl through the center of the cir needle so that the WS of the cowl is on the outside; the working yarn will be attached to what is now the first st on the left needle tip.

NEXT RND: Yo, k13 for right sleeve, pm, k31 for front, pm, k13 for left sleeve, pm, k30 for back, knit the last back st tog with the yo at the beg of the rnd to close the hole where the cowl was turned inside out, pm for end-of-rnd—88 sts; rnd begins at right back raglan.

INC RND: K1f&b (see Glossary), *knit to 1 st before m, k1f&b, slip marker (sl m), k1f&b; rep from * 2 more times, knit to last st, k1f&b—8 sts inc'd, 1 st each side of each of the 4 raglan markers.

Knit 1 (1, 0, 0, 0) rnd even. Cont in St st, rep inc rnd every rnd 0 (0, 3, 7, 14) times, then every other rnd 8 (17, 22, 22, 20) times, then every 3rd rnd 8 (3, 0, 0, 0) times, changing to size 7

(4.5 mm) 36″ (90 cm) needle when sts no longer fit comfortably around shorter cir needle—224 (256, 296, 328, 368) sts; 65 (73, 83, 91, 101) sts each for back and front; 47 (55, 65, 73, 83) sts for each sleeve; piece measures about 7 (7½, 8, 8¾, 9¼)″ (18 [19, 20.5, 22, 23.5] cm) from last rib rnd of cowl measured straight up along a single column of knit sts (do not measure along diagonal raglan lines).

DIVIDE FOR BODY AND SLEEVES

Place first 47 (55, 65, 73, 83) sts for right sleeve on a holder. With smooth waste yarn and using a provisional method (see Glossary), CO 8 sts onto left needle tip. Removing raglan markers as you come to them and using main yarn, knit 4 new CO sts, pm for right side "seam," knit rem 4 new CO sts, k65 (73, 83, 91, 101) front sts. Place next 47 (55, 65, 73, 83) sts for left sleeve on a holder. With smooth waste yarn, provisionally CO 8 sts onto left needle tip. Removing raglan m as you come to them, knit 4 new CO sts, pm for left side "seam," knit rem 4 new CO sts, k65 (73, 83, 91, 101) back sts, knit first 4 new CO sts again to end at right side seam m—146 (162, 182, 198, 218) sts total; 73 (81, 91, 99, 109) sts each for front and back between side markers. Work even in St st in the rnd until piece measures 4 (4½, 5, 5½, 6)″ (10 [11.5, 12.5, 14, 15] cm) from dividing rnd, or until piece just covers the bust snugly. Place 73 (81, 91, 99, 109) front sts on holder.

Lower Back

Working 73 (81, 91, 99, 109) back sts back and forth in rows, work even in St st until piece measures about 13″ (33 cm) from where back and front split (for all sizes) and about 17 (17½, 18, 18½, 19)″ (43 [44.5, 45.5, 47, 48.5] cm) from where body and sleeves divided, or about ¾″ (2 cm) less than desired total length from underarm to lower edge, ending with a RS row.

RIGHT SIDE INSERT

With RS of back still facing, pick up and knit 51 sts along right back selvedge to where front and back split.

NEXT ROW: (WS) K2tog, k1, *p2, k2; rep from * to end—50 sts rem.

Work short-rows on 50 insert sts only, turning at the end of each short-row without wrapping any sts at the turning point as foll:

SHORT-ROW 1: (RS) Sl 1 pwise wyb, p1, *k2, yo, p2tog; rep from * to last 4 sts, k2, turn, leaving last 2 sts unworked.

SHORT-ROW 2: (WS) Yo, work sts as they appear to last st, knitting each yo of rib patt and working sl st at end of row as k1.

42″
106.5 cm

9″
23 cm

19½″
49.5 cm

12¼ (14, 16¼, 18, 20¼)″
31 (35.5, 41.5, 45.5, 51.5) cm

13″
33

7 (7½, 8, 8¾, 9¼)″
18 (19, 20.5, 22, 23.5) cm

Front & Back

4 (4½, 5, 5½, 6)″
10 (11.5, 12.5, 14, 15) cm

32½ (36, 40¼, 44, 48½)″
82.5 (91.5, 103, 112, 123) cm

27½″
70 cm

13¾″
35 cm

18½ (18½, 19, 19, 19½)″
47 (47, 48.5, 48.5, 49.5) cm

41 (44¼, 49, 52½, 57)″
104 (113, 124.5, 133.5, 145) cm

SHORT-ROW 3: Sl 1 pwise, p1, *k2, yo, p2tog; rep from * to 4 sts before previous turning point (not including yo), turn.

SHORT-ROW 4: Yo, work sts as they appear to last st, k1.

SHORT-ROWS 5-22: Rep Short-rows 3 and 4 nine more times—8 sts rem before previous turning point with RS facing.

SHORT-ROW 23: Sl 1 pwise, p1, k2, turn.

SHORT-ROW 24: Yo, p2, k2.

SHORT-ROW 25: (RS) Sl 1 pwise, p1, *k2, purl turning point yo tog with st after it, p1; rep from * to end—50 sts; insert measures about 4¼" (11 cm) from pick-up row at beg of RS rows. Cut yarn and place 50 insert sts on holder. Place 73 (81, 91, 99, 109) back sts on separate holder.

Lower Front

Return 73 (81, 91, 99, 109) held front sts to size 7 (4.5 mm) 36" (90 cm) cir needle and rejoin yarn with RS facing. Working back and forth in rows, work even in St st until piece measures about 13" (33 cm) for all sizes from where back and front split and about 17 (17½, 18, 18½, 19)" (43 [44.5, 45.5, 47, 48.5] cm) from where body and sleeves divided, or about ¾" (2 cm) less than desired total length from underarm to lower edge, ending with a RS row.

LEFT SIDE INSERT

With RS of front still facing, pick up and knit 51 sts along left front selvedge to where front and back split. Work as for right side insert, ending with RS Short-row 25—50 sts. Leave sts on needle. Do not cut yarn.

Join Sides

With RS facing and beg at top of left split where back and front divided, pick up and knit 51 sts along left back selvedge, ending at lower edge.

NEXT ROW: (WS) Purl to last 2 sts, p2tog—50 sts.

Break yarn. Place 50 sts from back selvedge on separate needle. With yarn threaded on a tapestry needle, use the Kitchener st (see Glossary) to graft the live insert sts tog with the picked-up sts to join front and back at left side. Return 50 held right side insert sts to size 7 (4.5 mm) 36" (90 cm) needle and rejoin yarn to end of these sts with RS facing. With RS still facing and

beg at top of right split where back and front divided, pick up and knit 51 sts along right front selvedge, ending at lower edge. Complete as for left side join.

Lower Edge Ribbing

With RS facing, rejoin yarn to end of 73 (81, 91, 99, 109) front sts still on size 7 (4.5 mm) 36" (90 cm) needle. With RS facing, pick up and knit 28 sts from selvedge of left side insert, return 73 (81, 91, 99, 109) back sts to needle and knit across them, then pick up and knit 28 sts from selvedge of right side insert—202 (218, 238, 254, 274) sts total. Pm and join for working in rnds.

NEXT RND: *K1, p1; rep from * to end.

Work 3 more rnds in rib as established—piece measures about 17¾ (18¼, 18¾, 19¼, 19¾)" (45 [46.5, 47.5, 49, 50] cm) from where body and sleeves divided. Using size 9 (5.5 mm) needle, loosely BO all sts in rib patt.

Sleeves

Place 47 (55, 65, 73, 83) held sleeve sts on size 7 (4.5 mm) 16" (40 cm) cir needle and rejoin yarn to end of these sts with RS facing. With smooth waste yarn, provisionally CO 8 sts onto left needle tip. Using main yarn, knit 4 new CO sts, pm for beg of rnd, knit rem 4 new CO sts, k47 (55, 65, 73, 83) sleeve sts, then knit first 4 new CO sts again to end at m—55 (63, 73, 81, 91) sts.

SIZE 32½" ONLY

Work even in St st until piece measures about 3¼ (8.5)" from underarm.

INC RND: Work a left-slant lifted inc in first st (see Glossary), knit to last st, work a right-slant lifted inc (see Glossary) in last st—57 sts.

Work even in St st until piece measures 6½" (16.5 cm) from underarm.

NEXT RND: M1, *p1, k1; rep from * to last st, p1—58 sts.

Work 6 more rnds in established rib, working inc'd st as k1. Skip to All Sizes below.

SIZES (36, 40½, 44, 48½)" ONLY

Work even in St st until piece measures about 1" (2.5 cm) from underarm.

DEC RND: K2tog, knit to last 2 sts, ssk—2 sts dec'd.

Rep the dec rnd every (24, 5, 3, 2) rnds (1, 6, 10, 15) more time(s)—59 sts for all sizes. Work even in St st until piece measures (6½, 7, 7, 7½)" ([16.5 18, 18, 19] cm) from underarm.

NEXT RND: K2tog, *p1, k1; rep from * to last st, p1—58 sts.

Work 6 more rnds in established rib.

ALL SIZES
Change to size 8 (5 mm) 16" (40 cm) cir needle and work 6 more rnds in established rib.

NEXT RND: *K1, yo, p1; rep from *—87 sts.

Beg with Rnd 2, work single eyelet rib (see Stitch Guide) for 6 rnds. Change to size 9 (5.5 mm) 16" (40 cm) needle and work as established for 5 more rnds.

NEXT RND: *K1, M1, p2; rep from *—116 sts.

Change to double eyelet rib and work 12 rnds total. Change to size 10 (6 mm) 16" (40 cm) needles and cont as established for 12 more rnds, ending with Rnd 2 of patt—sleeve measures about 12" (30.5 cm) from beg of rib patts and 18½ (18½, 19, 19, 19½)" (47 [47, 48.5, 48.5, 49.5] cm) from underarm. Loosely BO all sts in k2, p2 rib.

Finishing

Block to measurements, being careful not to stretch garment when wet. Carefully remove waste yarn from provisional CO of body and sleeves at underarms and place live sts on separate needles. With yarn threaded on a tapestry needle, use the Kitchener st to graft sleeves and body tog at underarms. Weave in loose ends.

TOP-DOWN SEAMLESS SET-IN SLEEVE CONSTRUCTION

Barbara Walker's description of seamless set-in sleeve construction in *Knitting from the Top* provides inspiration as well as in-depth detail for this intriguing technique. It gives knitters who love seamless construction the means to achieve the sophisticated look of made-in-pieces sweaters without the tricky and often frustrating armhole seams. This construction technique is especially useful for sweaters worked in solid colors or with fine-gauge yarns, where poorly sewn seams are obvious. I have experimented with two of the three methods Barbara Walker recommends for creating seamless set-in sleeves—working the body and sleeves simultaneously and working the body and sleeves separately. Both give excellent re-

sults. The sweaters in this book that are worked from the top down with set-in sleeve construction are Anjou (page 24) and Viola (page 112).

Simultaneous Body and Sleeves

This method has an elegant simplicity that knitters of all skill levels can achieve. I'm partial to this method because it gives a smooth look, requires that only a few stitches be picked up at the top of the shoulder (rather than around the entire armhole), and produces a tidy, almost invisible seam line, depending on the type of increase.

For this method, the sweater begins at the shoulder line with a provisional cast-on for the entire width of the shoulders. This approach lets the work progress in two directions—down the front and down the back. You work the front and back separately, with short-rows worked across the back to add a bit more fabric at the back neckline (Figure 1), until each measures about a third of the way to

FIGURE 1

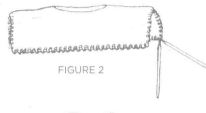

FIGURE 2

FIGURE 3

FIGURE 4

the underarms. You then join front and back as you pick up stitches for the sleeves at each armhole edge (Figure 2).

For a pullover, work across the front stitches, pick up stitches for the left sleeve, work across the back, pick up stitches for the right sleeve, then join for working in rounds. For a cardigan or a pullover with a low neckline, the row begins at the left front and ends at the right front. Continue to

TIPS FOR TOP-DOWN SET-IN CONSTRUCTION

- Working the body and sleeves simultaneously uses the tortoise-and-hare lesson of "slow and steady wins the race." Don't be discouraged by the relatively slow progress in the beginning when there are so many stitches on the needles. You will pick up speed after you divide the body and sleeves.

- The first and last stitches you pick up for the sleeves have a tendency to stretch and create "jogs" in the seam lines. You'll be able to minimize these jogs with blocking.

- Always use your blocked gauge swatch to get the best idea of how your yarn will behave after finishing and blocking.

- When you work the body and sleeves separately, pay particular attention to the depth of the armhole. An overly long armscye will result in a larger upper sleeve width. To check the fit, pin the front and back together under the arms (hook a few safety pins together in a chain to span wide widths) to determine the optimum depth. Then cast on the necessary number of stitches for the underarm, keeping in mind that these stitches will add to the sleeve width. It's also a good idea to measure your work against an existing garment that fits well.

- To keep the sleeves from being too wide at the base of the armholes, use short-rows to create smooth, narrow sleeve caps. Doing so eliminates the problem—inherent in raglan constructions—of overly generous sleeves.

- The key to a perfect fit is to try on the garment along the way. Although it's awkward at first when there isn't much knitted fabric, the inconvenience far outweighs the disappointment of an ill-fitting sweater.

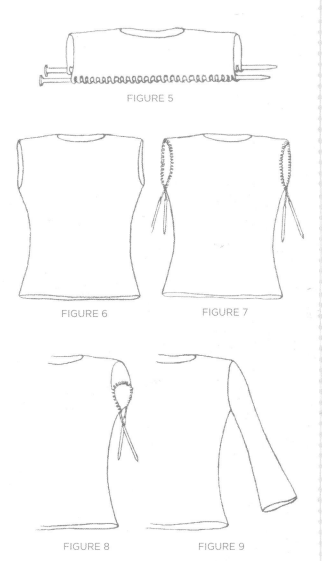

FIGURE 5

FIGURE 6

FIGURE 7

FIGURE 8

FIGURE 9

work the body and sleeves together to the base of the armholes (Figure 3). From this point on, you work the garment the same way as a top-down raglan (see page 54). You knit the body down to the hem, shaping the bust, waist, and hips along the way, and you knit the sleeves down to the cuffs, using decreases to create the desired taper (Figure 4).

Separate Body and Sleeves

With this method, you work the body first, then pick up stitches around the completed armholes for the sleeves. Like the simultaneous-body-and-sleeves method, this method begins with a provisional cast-on at the shoulders. You work the front and back separately to the underarms, again adding short-rows to the back for shaping (Figure 5). You then work increases to produce a gentle curve along the lower armhole edges. Though worked in reverse, the resulting shape is the same as that produced for set-in sleeve garments worked from the bottom up.

At the base of the armholes, you join the front and back for working in rounds to the hem, shaping the bust, waist, and hips along the way (Figure 6). You pick up stitches around the armholes (Figure 7) and work each sleeve in rounds to the cuff, beginning with a few plain rounds, followed by a good supply of short-rows to shape the shoulder area of the cap (Figure 8). As for any type of top-down construction, you work the sleeve to the cuff and shape it with decreases along the way (Figure 9).

dans LA RUE

STREETWEAR WITH STYLE

One night in Paris, under a moody October sky, the twinkling monuments were lit from dusk to dawn, and admission to them was free. We had happily stumbled onto the first of a now-yearly event, *Nuit Blanche*. This "white night," which is what the French call a sleepless night, involved the entire town. Everyone was awake and strolling the avenues. Musicians serenaded us as we walked; grandmothers with their *petites* in tow smiled and wished us a fond *bonsoir*; shops were open; artisans still labored at their crafts in miniature ateliers, their faces illuminated like Renaissance paintings. We were transfixed and fought off tiredness to join them. There was an atmosphere of such joy and love for this City of Light. We were reminded how strong the power of communal experience is, something Europeans have long celebrated.

This love of shared exchange is in its full glory on market day. In countless villages throughout France, young and old are up at dawn, greeting friends, discussing the latest recipes with their favorite vendors, sampling a bit of *fromage*, and finally stopping for the little *verre* at the neighborhood watering hole. Given the vibrant lifestyle, the elders are especially sprightly, something I'm constantly reminded of as they speed past me up a cobblestone walkway, often carting overflowing shopping bags home for the all-important midday meal.

For Dans la Rue, the look is *decontracté*, or relaxed, something you could slip on at a moment's notice with a favorite pair of jeans, such as Bijou, or use to dress up a basic black frock, such as the minimalist shrug Véronique. Techniques are kept simple, yet the designs themselves aren't simplistic. You can experiment with many types of seamless construction, maybe dabble in a bit of easy lace on large needles, as with Louisa, or slip-stitch colorwork, as with Martine. I hope you enjoy knitting these garments as much as I delighted in designing them. And perhaps we will meet someday *dans la rue*.

VIOLA * *short-sleeved cardigan*

Stringed instruments hold a special place in my life. Once upon a time, my husband and I were itinerant musicians. It wasn't that we lacked a home; we were simply on a journey to a place we hadn't yet found. Along the way we played music on the street for a bit of money to propel our crusty Dodge van just one mile farther.

We actually met each other on the street, or more correctly the road, a wide esplanade in Santa Barbara called "The Green," where hitchhikers gathered in hopes of a ride north. When the van in which he was riding pulled up, he jumped out, guitar in hand. I jumped in, also toting a guitar. To this day, I bless whatever force pushed him back into that van and my life.

Viola was named for the stringed instrument whose curvaceous shape inspired its silhouette and whose rich wood called for the wine-deep tint of the yarn. Add floaty edgings to this top-down set-in sleeve beauty if you wish or keep it as clean and simple as a well-played sonata.

FINISHED SIZE

32 (36½, 40, 44½, 48)" (81.5 [92.5, 101.5, 113, 122] cm) bust circumference. Sweater shown measures 32" (81.5 cm).

YARN

Worsted weight (#4 Medium) and sport-weight (#2 Fine).

SHOWN HERE: Rowan Kidsilk Aura (75% kid mohair, 25% silk; 82 yd [75 m]/25 g): #762 damson (MC; dark plum), 6 (7, 8, 9, 10) skeins.

Rowan Kidsilk Night (67% kid mohair, 18% silk, 10% polyester, 5% nylon; 227 yd [208 m]/25 g): #608 moonlight (CC; light gray), 1 skein for all sizes. NOTE: Kidsilk Night has been discontinued; substitute the laceweight mohair/silk yarn of your choice.

NEEDLES

BODY AND SLEEVES: size U.S. 10½ (6.5 mm): 16" and 36" (40 and 90 cm) circular (cir). SLEEVE PICK-UP, FRONT BANDS, CUFFS, AND RUFFLES: size U.S. 7 (4.5 mm): 16" and 24" (60 cm) cir. NECK EDGING BIND-OFF: size U.S. 11 (13 mm). *Adjust needle size if necessary to obtain the correct gauge.*

NOTIONS

Stitch holders or waste yarn for holders; smooth waste yarn for provisional CO; markers (m); tapestry needle; size G/6 (4.25 mm) crochet hook; five ⅜" (1 cm) buttons.

GAUGE

14 stitches and 20 rows = 4" (10 cm) in stockinette stitch using MC on size 10½ (6.5 mm) needles, after light blocking.

Shoulders

BACK

With longer size 10½ (6.5 mm) cir needle, smooth waste yarn, and using a provisional method (see Glossary), CO 40 (46, 52, 56, 60) sts. Join MC with WS facing.

NEXT ROW: (WS) P8 (11, 14, 16, 18) for right shoulder, place marker (pm), p24 for back neck, pm, p8 (11, 14, 16, 18) for left shoulder.

Shape back neck using short-rows, turning at the end of each short-row without wrapping any sts at the turning point as foll:

SHORT-ROW 1: (RS) K8 (11, 14, 16, 18), slip marker (sl m), k3, turn.

SHORT-ROW 2: (WS) Yo, purl to end.

SHORT-ROW 3: Knit to end, knitting yo tog with the st after it as k2tog.

SHORT-ROW 4: P8 (11, 14, 16, 18), sl m, p3, turn.

SHORT-ROW 5: Yo, knit to end.

SHORT-ROW 6: Purl across all sts, purling yo tog with the st after it as ssp (see Glossary).

Work even in St st on all sts for 10 more rows, ending with a WS row—piece measures about 3″ (7.5 cm) from CO at selvedges and about 2½″ (6.5 cm) from CO at center back. Leave yarn attached at left back armhole edge and place sts on holder.

RIGHT FRONT

Hold back piece with RS facing and provisional CO across the top. Carefully remove waste yarn of provisional CO from 8 (11, 14, 16, 18) sts at beg of row and place live sts on size 10½ (6.5 mm) cir needle for right shoulder. With RS facing, mark first st with waste yarn to indicate shoulder line at armhole edge. Join MC with WS facing and work in St st for 5 rows, beg and ending with a WS row.

NECK INC ROW: (RS) Knit to last st, work a left-slant lifted inc (see Glossary) in last st—1 st inc'd at neck edge.

Work 5 rows even, rep neck inc row, then work 3 rows even, ending with a WS row—10 (13, 16, 18, 20) sts; piece measures about 3″ (7.5 cm) from marked shoulder line. Leave yarn attached at right armhole edge and place sts on holder.

LEFT FRONT

Hold back piece with RS facing and provisional CO across the top. Carefully remove waste yarn of provisional CO from 8 (11, 14, 16, 18) sts at end of row and place live sts on size 10½ (6.5 mm) cir needle for left shoulder. With RS facing, mark last st with waste yarn to indicate shoulder line at armhole edge. Join a new ball of MC with WS facing and work in St st for 5 rows, beg and ending with a WS row.

NECK INC ROW: (RS) Work a right-slant lifted inc (see Glossary) in first st, knit to end—1 st inc'd at neck edge.

Work 5 rows even, rep neck inc row, then work 2 rows even, ending with a RS row—10 (13, 16, 18, 20) sts; piece measures about 3″ (7.5 cm) from shoulder line marker. Leave sts on needle. Do not cut yarn.

JOIN SHOULDERS AND SLEEVES

With RS facing and using yarn attached at end of left front sts, use a size 7 (4.5 mm) needle to pick up and knit 9 sts along left front armhole edge to shoulder line, then 9 sts along left back armhole selvedge from shoulder line to held back sts, cut yarn—18 left sleeve sts on smaller needle. Return 40 (46, 52, 56, 60) held back sts to size 10½ (6.5 mm) needle with RS facing and, using yarn attached to right back armhole and larger needle, knit across back sts. With RS still facing and using yarn attached to end of back sts, use a second size 7 (4.5 mm) needle to pick up and knit 9 sts along right back armhole edge to shoulder line, then 9 sts along right front armhole selvedge from shoulder line to held right front sts, break yarn—18 right sleeve sts on smaller needle. Return 10 (13, 16, 18, 20) held right front sts to size 10½ (6.5 mm)

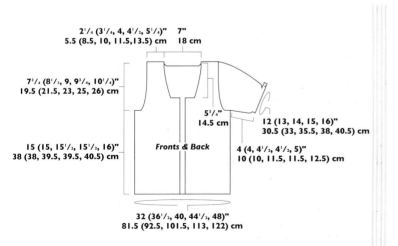

2¼ (3¼, 4, 4½, 5¼)"
5.5 (8.5, 10, 11.5,13.5) cm

7"
18 cm

7¾ (8½, 9, 9¾, 10¼)"
19.5 (21.5, 23, 25, 26) cm

5¼"
14.5 cm

12 (13, 14, 15, 16)"
30.5 (33, 35.5, 38, 40.5) cm

15 (15, 15½, 15½, 16)"
38 (38, 39.5, 39.5, 40.5) cm

Fronts & Back

4 (4, 4½, 4½, 5)"
10 (10, 11.5, 11.5, 12.5) cm

32 (36½, 40, 44½, 48)"
81.5 (92.5, 101.5, 113, 122) cm

needle with RS facing and, using yarn attached to right front armhole and larger needle, knit across right front sts—18 sleeve sts
each on two separate smaller needles; sts for fronts and back on
one larger needle separated by the groups of sleeve sts.

NEXT ROW: (WS) Using size 10½ (6.5 mm) needle for entire row,
p10 (13, 16, 18, 20) right front sts, pm, p18 right sleeve sts, pm,
p40 (46, 52, 56, 60) back sts, pm, p18 left sleeve sts, pm, p10 (13,
16, 18, 20) left front sts—96 (108, 120, 128, 136) sts total.

Upper Body and Sleeves

ROW 1: (RS, sleeve and neck inc row) Work a right-slant lifted inc
in first st at left neck edge, *knit to sleeve m, sl m, work a left-
slant lifted inc, knit to 1 st before next sleeve m, work a right-slant
lifted inc in last sleeve st, sl m; rep from * once more, knit to last
st, work a left-slant lifted inc in last st at right neck edge—6 sts
inc'd; 1 st inc'd for each front, 2 sts inc'd for each sleeve.

EVEN-NUMBERED ROWS 2-12: (WS) Purl.

ROWS 3 AND 5: (RS, sleeve inc row) *Knit to sleeve m, sl m, work a left-slant lifted inc, knit to 1 st before next sleeve m, work a right-slant lifted inc in last sleeve st, sl m; rep from * once more, knit to end—4 sts inc'd; 2 sts inc'd for each sleeve in each row.

ROW 7: Rep Row 1.

ROWS 9, 11, AND 13: Rep Row 3—128 (140, 152, 160, 168) sts after completing Row 13; 12 (15, 18, 20, 22) sts each front; 40 (46, 52, 56, 60) back sts; 32 sts each sleeve.

ROW 14: Purl—back and fronts measure about 5¾" (14.5 cm) from marked shoulder line.

ROW 15: Using the cable method (see Glossary), CO 6 sts at left front edge at beg of row, work to end as for Row 3.

ROW 16: Using the cable method, CO 6 sts at right front edge at beg of row, purl to end—144 (156, 168, 176, 184) sts; 18 (21, 24, 26, 28) sts each front; 40 (46, 52, 56, 60) back sts; 34 sts each sleeve.

Rep Rows 3 and 4 two (three, four, five, five) more times—152 (168, 184, 196, 204) sts; 18 (21, 24, 26, 28) sts each front, 40 (46, 52, 56, 60) back sts, 38 (40, 42, 44, 44) sts each sleeve.

NEXT ROW: (RS) Knit to 1 st before sleeve m, work a right-slant lifted inc in last left front st, *sl m, work a left-slant lifted inc, knit to 1 st before next sleeve m, work a right-slant lifted inc in last sleeve st, sl m,* work a left-slant inc in first back st, knit to last back st, work a right-slant inc in last back st; rep from * to * once more for right sleeve, work a left-slant inc in first right front st, knit to end—8 sts inc'd; 1 st inc'd for each front, 2 sts inc'd for back, 2 sts inc'd for each sleeve.

Purl 1 WS row. Cont in St st, rep the shaping of the last 2 rows 1 (2, 2, 3, 4) more time(s)—168 (192, 208, 228, 244) sts; 20 (24, 27, 30, 33) sts each front; 44 (52, 58, 64, 70) back sts; 42 (46, 48, 52, 54) sts each sleeve; fronts and back measure about 7¾ (8½, 9, 9¾, 10¼)" (19.5 [21.5, 23, 25, 26] cm) from marked shoulder line; sleeves measure about 4¾ (5½, 6, 6¾, 7¼)" (12 [14, 15, 17, 18.5] cm) from pick-up row in middle of sleeve cap measured straight up at center sleeve.

DIVIDE FOR BODY AND SLEEVES

K20 (24, 27, 30, 33) left front sts, place next 42 (46, 48, 52, 54) sts on holder for left sleeve, *with smooth waste yarn and using a provisional method, CO 8 (8, 8, 10, 10) sts onto left needle tip, with MC knit 4 (4, 4, 5, 5) new CO sts, pm for side "seam," knit

rem 4 (4, 4, 5, 5) new CO sts,* k44 (52, 58, 64, 70) back sts, place next 42 (46, 48, 52, 54) sts for right sleeve on a holder; rep from * to * once more for right underarm, k20 (24, 27, 30, 33) right front sts—100 (116, 128, 144, 156) sts total; 24 (28, 31, 35, 38) sts each front; 52 (60, 66, 74, 80) back sts.

Lower Body

Work 1 WS row even.

INC ROW: (RS) *Knit to 1 st before side m, work right-slant lifted inc in next st, sl m, work left-slant lifted inc in next st; rep from * once more—4 sts inc'd; 1 st inc'd for each front, 2 sts inc'd for back.

Work 1 WS row even, then rep inc row once more—108 (124, 136, 152, 164) sts; 26 (30, 33, 37, 40) sts each front; 56 (64, 70, 78, 84) back sts. Work even in St st until piece measures 15 (15, 15½, 15½, 16)" (38 [38, 39.5, 39.5, 40.5] cm) from underarm or desired total length, ending with a WS row. BO all sts with RS facing, leaving the last BO loop at bottom right front corner on needle.

BUTTONHOLE BAND

Transfer loop rem from lower edge BO to longer size 7 (4.5 mm) needle. With RS facing and smaller needle, pick up and knit 54 (56, 60, 62, 66) sts (about 2 sts for every 3 rows) along right front edge from lower corner to sts CO at base of right front neck—55 (57, 61, 63, 67) sts. Work 2 rows even in St st, ending with a RS row.

BUTTONHOLE ROW: (WS) P3, BO 1 st, *purl until there are 8 (9, 10, 11, 12) sts on right needle after BO gap, BO 1 st; rep from * once more, purl to end—3 buttonhole gaps.

NEXT ROW: (RS) Knit, using the backward-loop method (see Glossary) to CO 1 st over each BO gap in previous row to complete buttonholes.

Work 3 rows even, ending with a WS row.

PICOT ROW: (RS) K2, *yo, k2tog; rep from * to last st, k1.

Work 3 rows even, ending with a WS row.

BUTTONHOLE ROW: (RS) K33 (33, 35, 35, 37), *BO 1 st, knit until there are 8 (9, 10, 11, 12) sts on right needle after BO gap; rep from * once more, BO 1 st, knit to end—3 buttonhole gaps.

NEXT ROW: (WS) Purl, using the backward-loop method to CO 1 st over each BO gap in previous row to complete buttonholes.

Work 2 rows even, ending with a WS row. BO all sts. Cut yarn, leaving a long tail. Fold band to WS along picot row and with tail threaded on a tapestry needle, sew BO edge of band invisibly to pick-up row on WS. With yarn threaded on a tapestry needle, work buttonhole st (see Glossary) around each buttonhole, sewing through both layers of band.

BUTTONBAND

With MC, longer size 7 (4.5 mm) needle, and RS facing, pick up and knit 55 (57, 61, 63, 67) sts evenly along left front from beg of neck shaping to lower edge. Work even in St st for 7 rows, beg and ending with a WS row. Work picot row as for right front band, then work 7 more rows in St st, ending with a WS row. BO all sts. Finish as for buttonhole band, omitting buttonhole stitching.

Sleeves

LEFT SLEEVE

Place 42 (46, 48, 52, 54) held left sleeve sts on shorter size 10½ (6.5 mm) needle. With RS facing, join MC to beg of 8 (8, 8, 10, 10) sts CO for left underarm. With RS facing, pick up and knit 4 (4, 4, 5, 5) sts to center of underarm CO sts, pm, pick up 4 (4, 4, 5, 5) more sts from CO, sl last picked-up st to left needle and knit it tog with first sleeve st, knit to last sleeve st, work last sleeve st tog with first picked-up st, k3 (3, 3, 4, 4) to end at m—48 (52, 54, 60, 62) sts. Knit 1 rnd.

INC RND: Work left-slant lifted inc in next st, knit to last st, work right-slant lifted inc in last st—2 sts inc'd.

Rep inc rnd every rnd 5 (5, 6, 6, 7) more times—60 (64, 68, 74, 78) sts. Work even in St st until piece measures 3 (3, 3½, 3½, 4)" (7.5 [7.5, 9, 9, 10] cm) from underarm.

NEXT RND: K0 (1, 3, 1, 3), [k3, k2tog] 12 (12, 12, 14, 14) times, k0 (3, 5, 3, 5)—48 (52, 56, 60, 64) sts rem.

Knit 1 rnd. Cut yarn.

Cuff

Change to shorter size 7 (4.5 mm) needle. Sl first 24 (26, 28, 30, 32) sts pwise without working them. Rejoin MC with RS facing to next st in center of sleeve, k48 (52, 56, 60, 64) sts to end where new yarn was attached, removing end-of-rnd m as you come to it, then use the cable method to CO 8 sts for buttonhole tab at end of row—56 (60, 64, 68, 72) sts. Working back and forth in rows, purl 1 WS row.

BUTTONHOLE ROW: (RS) Knit to last 4 sts, BO 1 st for buttonhole, knit to end.

NEXT ROW: (WS) Purl to buttonhole gap, use the cable method to CO 1 st over buttonhole gap to complete buttonhole, purl to end.

Knit 1 RS row. BO all sts, leaving the last BO loop on needle—sleeve measures about 4 (4, 4½, 4½, 5)" (10 [10, 11.5, 11.5, 12.5] cm) from underarm. Place loop on crochet hook. With RS facing, work 1 row of single crochet (sc; see Glossary for crochet instructions) along the buttonhole tab selvedge, across the base of the sts CO for tab, and up the rem selvedge of tab opening to BO edge of sleeve. Fasten off last st. With yarn threaded on a tapestry needle, work buttonhole st around buttonhole.

RIGHT SLEEVE

Place 42 (46, 48, 52, 54) sts of second sleeve on shorter size 10½ (6.5 mm) needle. With RS facing, join MC to beg of 8 (8, 8, 10, 10) sts CO for right underarm. Work as for right sleeve to start of cuff.

Cuff

Change to shorter size 7 (4.5 mm) needle. Sl first 24 (26, 28, 30, 32) sts pwise without working them. Rejoin MC with RS facing to next st in center of sleeve, use the cable method to CO 8 sts for buttonhole tab onto left needle, knit across the 8 new sts, k48 (52, 56, 60, 64) sts to end where new yarn was attached, removing end-of-rnd m as you come to it—56 (60, 64, 68, 72) sts. Working back and forth in rows, purl 1 WS row.

BUTTONHOLE ROW: (RS) K3, BO 1 st for buttonhole, knit to end.

NEXT ROW: (WS) Purl to buttonhole gap, use the cable method to CO 1 st over buttonhole gap to complete buttonhole, purl to end.

Knit 1 RS row. BO all sts, leaving the last BO loop on needle. Place loop on crochet hook. With RS facing, work 1 row of sc down selvedge of tab opening, across the base of sts CO for tab, and up the buttonhole tab selvedge to BO edge of sleeve. Fasten off last st. With yarn threaded on a tapestry needle, work buttonhole st around buttonhole.

Finishing

NECK EDGING

Join MC to picot fold line of right front buttonhole band at neck edge. With size 7 (4.5 mm) needle and RS facing, pick up and knit 34 sts long right front neck, picking up through both layers of buttonhole band, carefully remove waste yarn of provisional CO from 24 back neck sts, place live sts on needle and knit across them inc 6 sts evenly to 30 sts as you go, then pick up and knit 34 sts along left front neck to picot fold line of button band, picking up through both layers of band—98 sts total for all sizes. Using size 11 (8 mm) needle, BO all sts on next WS row.

Wet-block garment to measurements, smoothing and straightening unfinished lower body edge and front bands.

SLEEVE RUFFLE (MAKE 2)

With CC and size 7 (4.5 mm) needle, CO 55 (61, 65, 69, 73) sts. Work even in St st for 10 rows. BO all sts firmly. With RS of both sleeve and ruffle facing up, position BO edge of ruffle underneath BO edge of cuff so that cuff overlaps ruffle by about ¼" (0.6 cm), and with ends of ruffle about 1" (2.5 cm) in from each end of cuff BO row, easing to fit. Pin selvedges of ruffle along outer 1" (2.5 cm) of cuff BO row at each side. With MC threaded on a tapestry needle, sew ruffle in place as invisibly as possible.

FRONT RUFFLE (MAKE 2)

With CC and size 7 (4.5 mm) needle, CO 30 sts. Work even in St st for 10 rows. BO all sts firmly. With RS of both front and front ruffle facing up, position BO edge of ruffle underneath neck edging so that neck overlaps ruffle by about ¼" (0.6 cm), with one end of ruffle about 3" (7.5 cm) down from shoulder line, the other end of ruffle aligned with pick-up row for front band, and easing to fit. Pin selvedges of ruffle to neck edge above ruffle at one end and to upper edge of front band at the other end. With MC threaded on a tapestry needle, sew ruffle in place as invisibly as possible.

Sew buttons to left front opposite buttonholes. Sew a button to each cuff, opposite buttonhole. Weave in loose ends. Block lightly to measurements again if desired, being careful not to flatten ruffles.

YARN SUBSTITUTIONS

Feel free to substitute yarns for those I've recommended in this book. The yarn world is brimming with closeouts, stash reductions, and budget options as well as non-animal/vegan choices. If you have time, consider repurposing and recycling the fabulous yarns in vintage sweaters. Check your local thrift store and Goodwill. You'd be surprised by the treasures they hold.

For successful substitutions, gauge alone shouldn't be the deciding factor. You'll want to pay close attention to the fiber content and weight of the recommended yarn, both of which are crucial for proper drape and final appearance. For example, a closely fitted dress, such as Nadine (page 40), originally created in bamboo/cotton blend yarn, would look stiff and unappealing in a coarse wool yarn knitted at the same gauge. Consider instead a silk blend or an animal-free yarn made of milk protein, hemp, linen, or soy, all of which would produce a similar effect. Clara Parkes's *The Knitter's Book of Yarn* is a valuable tool for bumping up your yarn IQ; the more you know, the easier it will be to find a suitable substitute.

Before settling on a substitution, knit a large swatch—at least 6" (15 cm) square—then wash it and observe what happens. Does it shrink, sag, or worse yet (and I learned this from experience), fall apart? If so, you'll want to look for another yarn. To help you get started, you'll find possible substitutions for each design in this book at the French Girl website (frenchgirlknits.com). To discover which yarns other knitters have used, check the project pages of Ravelry (ravelry.com). Thanks to the Internet, we have a worldwide community of knitters who love to share their successes (and are willing to share their failures).

MARTINE ✳ *slip-stitch bordered hoodie*

Ｆrench sailors have the most adorable outfits (although I wouldn't say so within their hearing). Men of the sea are central to my family's history: father, uncle, and grandfather all sailed and farmed our bay on the Washington coast. My Cajun ancestors punted their *bateaux* through bayou country, and I learned recently that their *grandpères* cruised waterways in the Poitou-Charente region of France long before they left for the shores of North America.

Martine has a distinct sailor influence, with a generous hood (for the hoodie generation) replacing the squared off middy collar. Though never a fan of acres of stockinette stitch, I knew that this particular design called out for an almost blank palette to throw the spotlight on the colorwork. If you harbor Fair Isle fear, the easily worked slip-stitch bands will give your confidence a boost. Subtle ribbing that hugs the lower torso definitely improves on roomy maritime gear while the spongy organic yarn ramps up the cozy factor times ten. Martine is perfect for misty morning trawling of your own.

FINISHED SIZE

32 (36, 39, 44, 47)" (81.5 [91.5, 99, 112, 119.5] cm) bust circumference. Sweater shown measures 32" (81.5 cm).

YARN

Worsted weight (#4 Medium).

SHOWN HERE: Vermont Organic Fiber Company O-Wool Classic (100% wool; 198 yd [181 ml]/100 g): #9102 black (MC), 4 (5, 5, 6, 7) balls; #4302 willow (A; light green), and #2301 cornflower (B), 1 ball each.

NEEDLES

YOKE AND LOWER BODY: size U.S. 9 (5.5 mm) 24" and 36" (60 and 90 cm) circular (cir). RIBBED LOWER BODICE AND HOOD: size U.S. 7 (4.5 mm) 24" (60 cm) cir. SLEEVE AND FRONT EDGINGS: size U.S. 8 (5 mm) 16" and 36" (40 and 90 cm) cir. PROVISIONAL CAST-ON AT NECK: size U.S. 7 (4.5 mm): straight. *Adjust needle size if necessary to obtain the correct gauge.*

NOTIONS

Stitch holders; markers (m); smooth cotton waste yarn for provisional cast-on; size G/6 (4.25 mm) crochet hook; tapestry needle.

GAUGE

16 stitches and 21½ rows/rounds = 4" (10 cm) in stockinette stitch on size 9 (5.5 mm) needle; 18 stitches and 23 rounds = 4" (10 cm) in p1, k2 rib on size 7 (4.5 mm) needle, with rib slightly stretched so p1 columns appear about ½ stitch wide; 17 stitches and 22 rows = 4" (10 cm) in stockinette stitch on size 7 (4.5 mm) needle; 17 stitches and 32 rows/rounds = 4" (10 cm) in slip-stitch patterns on size 8 (5 mm) needle.

Notes

The yoke is worked in one piece from the neck edge down to the underarms where stitches are put on holders for the cap sleeves. The front and back are worked in the round in one piece to the lower edge. The hood is worked upward from the provisional cast-on at the neck, and then the cap-sleeve edgings and front placket edging are worked in a slip-stitch pattern.

When working back and forth in rows, slip the first st of all RS rows as if to purl with yarn in back, and slip the first st of all WS rows as if to purl with yarn in front, unless otherwise specified.

The circumference shown on the schematic for the ribbed hip area will stretch to about 2" to 3" (5 to 7.5 cm) larger than the bust measurement for the same size.

Stitch Guide

KRB

Knit into st in the row below the next st on left needle—1 st inc'd.

PRB

Purl into st in the row below the next st on left needle—1 st inc'd.

Yoke

With crochet hook, waste yarn, size 7 (4.5 mm) straight needle, and using the crochet-on method (see Glossary), provisionally CO 52 (60, 60, 64, 64) sts. Change to MC and shorter size 9 (5.5 mm) cir needle. Work back and forth in rows as foll: (WS) P8 (9, 9, 10, 10) for right front, place marker (pm) for right front raglan, p8 (10, 10, 10, 10) for right sleeve, pm for right back raglan, p20 (22, 22, 24, 24) for back, pm for left back raglan, p8 (10, 10, 10, 10) for left sleeve, pm for left front raglan, p8 (9, 9, 10, 10) for left front.

INC ROW: (RS) Sl 1 (see Notes), *knit to 1 st before m, k1f&b (see Glossary), slip marker (sl m), k1f&b; rep from 3 more times, knit to end—8 sts inc'd, 1 st on each side of all 4 raglan m.

NEXT ROW: (WS) Sl 1, purl to end.

Cont in St st with slipped edge sts, rep the last 2 rows 14 (16, 19, 22, 25) more times, changing to longer size 9 (5.5 cm) cir needle if there are too many sts to fit around the shorter needle—172 (196, 220, 248, 272) sts; 23 (26, 29, 33, 36) sts each front; 50 (56, 62, 70, 76) back sts; 38 (44, 50, 56, 62) sts each sleeve.

DIVIDE FOR BODY AND SLEEVES

(RS) Removing raglan m as you come to them, k23 (26, 29, 33, 36) for left front, place next 38 (44, 50, 56, 62) sts on holder for left sleeve, *use the crochet-on method, waste yarn, and size 7 (4.5 mm) needle to CO 10 (12, 12, 14, 14) sts for left underarm, with MC knit first 5 (6, 6, 7, 7) new CO sts, pm for side, knit rem 5 (6, 6, 7, 7) new CO sts,* k50 (56, 62, 70, 76) for back, place next 38 (44, 50, 56, 62) sts on holder for right sleeve; rep from * to * for right underarm, k23 (26, 29, 33, 36) for right front—116 (132, 144, 164, 176) sts total; 28 (32, 35, 40, 43) sts each front; 60 (68, 74, 84, 90) back sts; piece measures about 6 (6³/₄, 7³/₄, 9, 10)" (15 [17, 19.5, 23, 25.5] cm) from CO.

Lower Body

Work 2 rows even in St st, ending with a RS row. Use the crochet-on method, waste yarn, and size 7 (4.5 mm) needle to CO 12 sts for base of front placket.

JOINING RND: With RS facing and changing to shorter size 9 (5.5 cm) needle if necessary for your size, use MC attached at end of last row to knit across 12 provisional CO sts for base of front placket opening, knit across right front sts, sl m, knit to end of back sts—128 (144, 156, 176, 188) sts total; 68 (76, 82, 92, 98) front sts; 60 (68, 74, 84, 90) back sts; rnd beg at right side m.

Work in St st in the rnd until piece measures 4¹/₂" (11.5 cm) from dividing row, dec 0 (2, 2, 0, 0) sts each on front and back in last rnd—128 (140, 152, 176, 188) sts; 68 (74, 80, 92, 98) front sts; 60 (66, 72, 84, 90) back sts.

RIBBED LOWER BODICE

Change to size 7 (4.5 mm) cir needle and gradually convert to p1, k2 rib patt as foll:

RND 1: K31 (34, 37, 43, 46), *place removable marker on needle, [p1, k2] 2 times, p1, place removable marker on needle,* k30 (33, 36, 42, 45), sl side m, k27 (30, 33, 39, 42); rep from * to * once more, k26 (29, 32, 38, 41)—7 marked rib sts as close to center as possible on both front and back.

RND 2: Reposition each removable m 3 sts farther out from the center—13 sts between each pair of removable m on both front and back. *Knit to removable m, sl m, [p1, k2] 4 times, p1, sl m; rep from * once more, knit to end.

RND 3: Reposition each removable m 3 sts farther out from the center—6 more sts between m than for previous rnd. [Knit to removable m, sl m, *p1, k2; rep from * to 1 st before removable m, p1, sl m] 2 times, knit to end.

Rep the last rnd 6 (7, 8, 10, 11) more times, moving removable m 3 sts farther out from center before working each rnd—55 (61, 67, 79, 85) rib sts between removable m on both front and back; 7 sts before and 6 sts after marked rib sts on front; 3 sts before

16 (18, 18, 19, 19)"
40.5 (45.5, 45.5, 48.5, 48.5) cm

2¹/₄"
5.5 cm

6 (6³/₄, 7³/₄, 9, 10)"
15 (17, 19.5, 23, 25.5) cm

12¹/₄ (13, 14, 16, 17)"
31 (33, 35.5, 40.5, 43) cm

32 (36, 39, 44, 47)"
81.5 (91.5, 99, 112, 119.5) cm

16 (16, 15¹/₄, 15¹/₄, 15)"
40.5 (40.5, 38.5, 38.5, 38) cm

Front & Back

29 (31¹/₂, 34¹/₄, 39¹/₂, 42¹/₄)"
73.5 (80, 87, 100.5, 107.5) cm

and 2 sts after marked rib sts on back; piece measures about 6 (6¼, 6½, 6¾, 7)" (15 [16, 16.5, 17, 18] cm) from dividing row.

NEXT RND: Taking out removable m as you come to them, p2tog, k2, *p1, k2; rep from * to last front st, temporarily sl last front st to right needle, remove side m, p2tog (last front st tog with first back st), replace side m, k2, **p1, k2; rep from ** to end—126 (138, 150, 174, 186) sts; 67 (73, 79, 91, 97) front sts; 59 (65, 71, 83, 89) back sts.

Work sts in established p1, k2 rib (knit the knits and purl the purls as they appear) for 4 (4, 0, 0, 0) rnds.

WAIST DEC RND: P1, k2tog, *p1, k2; rep from * to last 4 front sts, p1, k2tog, p1, sl m, k2tog, **p1, k2; rep from ** to last 3 back sts,

p1, k2tog—4 sts dec'd; 122 (134, 146, 170, 182) sts total, 65 (71, 77, 89, 95) front sts, 57 (63, 69, 81, 87) back sts.

Work sts as they appear for 12 (12, 10, 8, 6) rnds—piece measures about 9¼ (9¼, 8½, 8½, 8¼)" (23.5 [23.5, 21.5, 21.5, 21] cm) from dividing row and 15¼ (16, 16¼, 17½, 18¼)" (38.5 [40.5, 41.5, 44.5, 46.5] cm) from CO at neck edge.

FIRST HIP INC RND: P1, krb (see Stitch Guide), k1, *p1, k2; rep from * to last 3 front sts, p1, krb, k1, p1, sl m, krb, k1, **p1, k2; rep from ** to last 2 back sts, p1, krb, k1—4 sts inc'd; 126 (138, 150, 174, 186) sts total, 67 (73, 79, 91, 97) front sts, 59 (65, 71, 83, 89) back sts.

Work in established p1, k2 rib for 12 rnds.

SECOND HIP INC RND: Krb, *p1, k2; rep from * to last front st, prb (see Stitch Guide), k1, sl m, prb, **k2, p1; rep from ** to last 2 back sts, k2, prb in rnd below first st of rnd, making sure last inc'd st stays in front of end-of-rnd m as part of the back sts—4 sts inc'd; 130 (142, 154, 178, 190) sts total, 69 (75, 81, 93, 99) front sts, 61 (67, 73, 85, 91) back sts.

Work sts as they appear for 25 rnds—piece measures about 16 (16, 15¼, 15¼, 15)" (40.5 [40.5, 38.5, 38.5, 38] cm) from dividing row, and about 22 (22¾, 23, 24¼, 25)" (56 [58, 58.5, 61.5, 63.5] cm) from CO at neck edge. BO all sts using the sewn method (see Glossary).

Hood

Block to measurements. Carefully remove waste yarn provisional CO at neck edge and place 52 (60, 60, 64, 64) live sts on size 7 (4.5 mm) cir needle. With RS facing, join MC to beg of sts at right neck. Work back and forth in rows as foll:

ROW 1: (RS) K2, p1, [k1, p1] 0 (1, 1, 2, 2) time(s), *[k1, p1] 3 (2, 2, 2, 2) times, k1, p2tog; rep from * to last 4 (6, 6, 8, 8) sts, [k1, p1] 1 (2, 2, 3, 3) time(s), k2—47 (53, 53, 57, 57) sts rem.

ROW 2: Sl 1, *p1, k1; rep from * to last 4 sts, p1, k1, p2.

ROW 3: Sl 1, *k1, p1; rep from * to last 4 sts, k1, p1, k2.

ROW 4: (WS) Sl 1, p0 (3, 3, 5, 5), *p5 (7, 7, 11, 11), prb, p1; rep from * to last 4 (9, 9, 15, 15) sts, p4 (4, 9, 9, 15, 15)—54 (58, 58, 60, 60) sts.

ROW 5: Sl 1, k20 (22, 22, 23, 23), krb, pm, k12, pm, krb, k21 (23, 23, 24, 24)—56 (60, 60, 62, 62) sts.

ROWS 6 AND 8: Sl 1, purl to end.

ROWS 7 AND 9: Sl 1, knit to m, krb, sl m, k12, sl m, krb, knit to end—60 (64, 64, 66, 66) sts after completing Row 9.

ROWS 10-14: Sl 1, work in St st to end.

ROW 15: Rep Row 7—2 sts inc'd.

ROWS 16-21: Rep Rows 10-15—64 (68, 68, 70, 70) sts.

ROWS 22-44: Sl 1, work in St st to end, ending with a WS row—piece measures about 8" (20.5 cm) from beg of hood.

ROW 45: Sl 1, knit to 2 sts before m, ssk, sl m, k12, sl m, k2tog, knit to end—2 sts dec'd.

ROWS 46-52: Sl 1, work in St st to end.

ROWS 53: Rep Row 45—2 sts dec'd.

ROWS 54-56: Sl 1, work in St st to end.

ROWS 57-68: Rep Rows 53-56 three more times—54 (58, 58, 60, 60) sts rem after Row 68.

ROW 69: Sl 1, knit to 2 sts before m, ssk, sl m, k4, ssk, pm in center of hood, k2tog, k4, sl m, k2tog, knit to end—50 (54, 54, 56, 56) sts.

ROWS 70-72: Sl 1, work in St st to end.

ROW 73: Sl 1, knit to 2 sts before m, ssk, sl m, knit to 2 sts before center m, ssk, sl m, k2tog, knit to m, sl m, k2tog, knit to end—4 sts dec'd.

ROW 74: Sl 1, work in St st to end.

ROWS 75-80: Rep Rows 73 and 74 three times—34 (38, 38, 40, 40) sts; piece measures about 14½" (37 cm) from beg of hood.

Cut yarn, leaving an 18" (45.5 cm) tail. Arrange sts evenly on 2 needles with 17 (19, 19, 20, 20) sts on each needle. Thread tail on a tapestry needle and use the Kitchener st (see Glossary) to graft the two halves of the hood tog.

Finishing

SLEEVE EDGING

Place 38 (44, 50, 56, 62) held sleeve sts on shorter size 8 (5 mm) cir needle. Carefully remove waste yarn from provisional CO sts at underarm and place 10 (12, 12, 14, 14) live sts on needle. With RS facing, sl sts without working them to the center of underarm CO sts and rejoin MC in middle of underarm.

NEXT RND: K5 (6, 6, 7, 7) underarm sts, k38 (44, 50, 56, 62) sleeve sts and at the same time inc 4 (inc 0, dec 2, dec 2, dec 4) sts evenly spaced, k5 (6, 6, 7, 7) CO sts, pm, and join for working in rnds—52 (56, 60, 68, 72) sts total.

Work slip-st patt in rnds as foll:

RND 1: With B, *k1, sl 1 as if to purl with yarn in back (pwise wyb); rep from *.

EVEN-NUMBERED RNDS 2-16: Knit with the same color used for previous rnd.

RND 3: With A, *k1, sl 1 pwise wyb; rep from *.

RND 5: With MC, *k1, sl 1 pwise with yarn in front (wyf); rep from *.

RND 7: With B, rep Rnd 1.

RND 9: With A, rep Rnd 5.

RND 11: With MC, rep Rnd 1.

RND 13: With B, rep Rnd 5.

RND 15: With A, rep Rnd 1.

RND 17: With MC, rep Rnd 5.

RND 18: With MC, knit—edging measures about 2¼" (5.5 cm).

With size 7 (4.5 mm) needle, BO all sts.

FRONT EDGING

With MC and size 7 (4.5 mm) cir needle, RS facing, and beg at lower right front corner of neck opening, pick up and knit 78 (80, 84, 88, 92) sts along right front opening to grafting row at top of hood (about 7 sts for every 10 rows) then 78 (80, 84, 88, 92) sts along left front opening from top of hood to lower left front corner—156 (160, 168, 176, 184) sts total. Change to longer size 8 (5 mm) cir needle and purl 1 WS row. Work slip-st patt in rows as foll:

ROW 1: (RS) With B, *k1, sl 1 pwise wyb; rep from *.

EVEN-NUMBERED ROWS 2–10: (WS) Purl with the same color used for previous row.

ROW 3: With A, *k1, sl 1 pwise wyb; rep from *.

ROW 5: With MC, *k1, sl 1 pwise wyf; rep from *.

ROW 7: With B, rep Row 1.

ROW 9: With A, rep Row 5.

ROW 11: With MC, rep Row 1.

ROW 12: With MC, *k1, p1; rep from *.

With size 9 (5.5 mm) needle, BO all sts. Carefully remove waste yarn from provisional CO sts at base of front placket opening and place 12 live sts on needle. With MC threaded on a tapestry needle, sew selvedges of front edging to sts CO at center front with BO edges of front touching in center, easing to fit. With MC threaded on a tapestry needle, sew BO edges of front opening tog at lower edge for desired length (about 1" [2.5 cm] for garment shown). Weave in loose ends. Block slip-st bands, if desired.

MARTINE

LOUISA ✳ *lace tunic*

FINISHED SIZE

36½ (39, 41¾, 44¼, 46¾)" (92.5 [99, 106, 112.5, 118.5] cm) bust circumference. Sweater shown measures 36½" (92.5 cm).

YARN

Chunky weight (#5 Bulky).

SHOWN HERE: Louisa Harding Thalia (52% nylon, 24% acrylic, 12% mohair, 6% wool, 6% metallic; 93 yd [85 m]/50 g): #8 Beauty (gold, plum, pink, tan mix), 5 (6, 7, 8, 9) skeins.

NEEDLES

SLEEVE AND LACE EDGINGS: size U.S. 11 (8 mm) 16" (40 cm) circular (cir). BODY AND YOKE: sizes U.S. 10½, 11, and 13 (6.5, 8, and 9 mm): 36" (90 cm) cir. NECK-LINE FINISHING: size U.S. 10 (6 mm): 24" (61 cm) cir. *Adjust needle size if necessary to obtain the correct gauge.*

NOTIONS

Markers (m); removable markers or safety pins; stitch holders or waste yarn; tapestry needle; 1½ yards (1.4 meters) ⅜" (1 cm) silk ribbon.

GAUGE

14 stitches and 22 rounds = 4" (10 cm) in stockinette stitch worked in rounds on size 10½ (6.5 mm) needle; 12½ stitches and 15½ rounds = 4" (10 cm) in lace pattern worked in rounds on size 13 (9 mm) needle; 14 stitches and 16 rounds = 4" (10 cm) in lace pattern worked in rows or rounds on size 11 (8 mm) needle.

One benefit of being in the knitting design world is meeting lovely kindred souls from all parts of the globe at yearly trade shows. Those gatherings could be rather soulless affairs without this communion. Double happiness occurs when someone has feminine über-delicious yarn and luscious designs that make every fiber of your French-Girl being sing with girly joy! "Yes, I will make a pink frothy dress," I thought when I spied this light confection of a yarn, even though I had recently sworn off anything remotely rosy.

Wanting a garment that was as unfussy in styling as the yarn was fluffy, the idea of using one continuous lace stitch in an A-line configuration, with shaping accomplished by changing needle size rather than decreasing stitches, seemed an elegant solution. Tiny doll-like sleeves and a ribbon-gathered neckline finished off this *petit four*, which is easily lengthened by adding rounds at the beginning.

In my garden grow peonies that are almost this shade of blush. Turn the opulent, just-picked flowers upside down and you can see how their ruffly edges became the scalloped stitches of Louisa. (Note to self: Stare at flowers often for inspiration.)

Notes

- To check gauge in lace pattern, cast on 20 stitches using the cable method and size 11 (8 mm) needles. Work the pattern back and forth in rows for 4" (10 cm), then measure your gauge. The finished bust measurement depends on getting the correct gauge using a size 11 (8 mm) needle.
- The sleeve edgings and lower body are worked separately to the armholes, then joined for working the yoke circularly in stockinette to the neck edge. The sleeve caps are shaped with short-rows.
- The sleeves shown are worked for a total of 6 lace rounds before joining at the yoke; for longer sleeves, work more 4-round pattern repeats, ending with Rnd 2 of the pattern.
- Plan on purchasing extra yarn if you lengthen the sleeves or lower body.

Stitch Guide

LACE PATTERN WORKED IN ROWS
(MULTIPLE OF 9 STS + 2)

ROW 1: (RS) K2, *yo, k2, k2togtbl, k2tog, k2, yo, k1; rep from * to end.

ROW 2: (WS) Purl.

ROW 3: K1, *yo, k2, k2togtbl, k2tog, k2, yo, k1; rep from * to last st, k1.

ROW 4: Purl.

Repeat Rows 1–4 for pattern.

LACE PATTERN WORKED IN ROUNDS
(MULTIPLE OF 9 STS + 2)

RND 1: K2, *yo, k2, k2togtbl, k2tog, k2, yo, k1; rep from * to end.

RND 2: Knit.

RND 3: K1, *yo, k2, k2togtbl, k2tog, k2, yo, k1; rep from * to last st, k1.

RND 4: Knit.

Rep Rnds 1–4 for pattern. NOTE: The pattern deliberately produces a 2-stitch column of knit stitches where the rounds change, with 1 knit stitch on each side of the end-of-round marker. For the sweater shown, this 2-stitch knit column is positioned at the center back.

Sleeves (make 2)

With shorter size 11 (8 mm) cir needle and using the cable method (see Glossary), CO 39 (48, 48, 57, 57) sts. Work Row 1 of lace patt worked in rows (see Stitch Guide) to the last st, place marker (pm), then join for working in rnds by knitting the last st tog with the first st (counts as first st of Rnd 2), being careful not to twist sts—38 (47, 47, 56, 56) sts. Cont lace patt worked in rnds (see Stitch Guide), work Rnds 2–4, then work Rnds 1 and 2 once more—6 patt rnds completed; piece measures about 1½" (3.8 cm) from CO (see Notes if making longer sleeves). Cut yarn. Place the last 4 sts and first 3 (3, 3, 4, 4) sts of the rnd on holder for underarm, then place rem 31 (40, 40, 48, 48) sts on separate holder for sleeve. Set aside.

Body

With size 13 (9 mm) cir needle and using the cable method, CO 129 (138, 147, 156, 165) sts. Work Row 1 of lace patt worked in rows to the last st, pm for end-of-rnd, then join for working in rnds by knitting the last st tog with the first st (counts as first st of Rnd 2), being careful not to twist sts—128 (137, 146, 155, 164) sts; rnd begins at center back. Work Rnds 2–4 of patt, then rep Rnds 1–4 of patt 10 (11, 12, 13, 14) more times—piece measures about 11¼ (12¼, 13½, 14½, 15½)" (28.5 [31, 34.5, 37, 39.5] cm) from CO. Change to size 11 (8 mm) cir needle and work Rnds

1–4 four times—piece measures about 15¼ (16¼, 17½, 18½, 19½)" (38.5 [41.5, 44.5, 47, 49.5] cm) from CO and about 5¾ (5¾, 6½, 6½, 7½)" (14.5 [14.5, 16.5, 16.5, 19] cm) below underarm. Try on garment to check length to underbust, and if necessary, work more 4-rnd patt reps to achieve desired length; every 4 rnds added will increase the overall length from CO to underarm by about 1" (2.5 cm). Change to size 10½ (6.5 mm) needle and work Rnds 1–4 of patt 2 times. Change to size 11 (8 mm) needle and rep Rnds 1–4 of patt 3 (3, 4, 4, 5) times, then work Rnds 1–3 once more—piece measures about 21 (22, 24, 25, 27)" (53.5 [56, 61, 63.5, 68.5] cm) from CO.

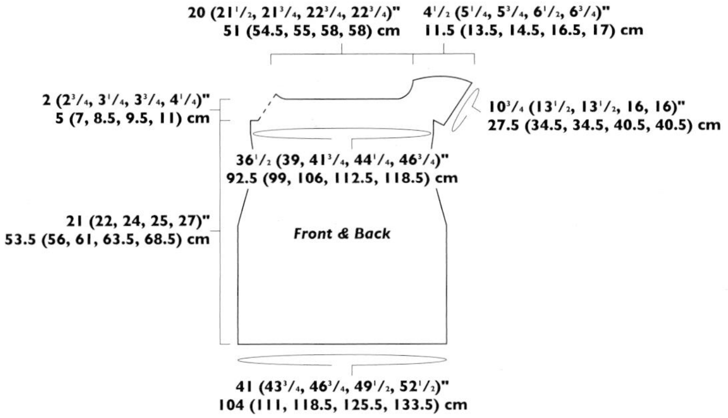

Yoke

Change to size 10½ (6.5 mm) cir needle. Work in St st as foll:

RND 1: Beg at center back, k28 (30, 33, 34, 37) left back sts, place next 7 (7, 7, 8, 8) sts on holder for left underarm, pm, k31 (40, 40, 48, 48) held left sleeve sts, pm, k58 (63, 66, 71, 74) front sts, place next 7 (7, 7, 8, 8) sts on holder for right underarm, pm, k31 (40, 40, 48, 48) held right sleeve sts, pm, k28 (30, 33, 34, 37) right back sts—176 (203, 212, 235, 244) sts total.

RND 2: *Knit to 2 sts before m, k3tog removing m and replacing it on needle after new dec st, knit to 1 st before next m, k3togtbl (see Glossary) removing m and replacing it on needle before new dec st; rep from * once more, knit to end—168 (195, 204, 227, 236) sts; 27 (29, 32, 33, 36) sts each for left and right back; 56 (61, 64, 69, 72) front sts; 29 (38, 38, 46, 46) sts for each sleeve.

RND 3: *Knit to 2 sts before m, k2tog, slip marker (sl m), knit to next marker, sl m, ssk; rep from * once more, knit to end—4 sts dec'd.

RND 4: *Knit to 2 sts before marker, p2tog, sl m, knit to next marker, sl m, p2togtbl; rep from * once more, knit to end—4 sts dec'd.

Rep the last rnd 3 (5, 6, 7, 9) more times—148 (167, 172, 191, 192) sts; 22 (22, 24, 24, 25) sts each for left and right back; 46 (47, 48, 51, 50) front sts; 29 (38, 38, 46, 46) sts each sleeve.

NEXT RND: *Knit to marker, sl m, p2togtbl, knit to 2 sts before next marked st, p2tog, sl m; rep from * once more, knit to end—144 (163, 168, 187, 188) sts; no change to back and front st counts; 27 (36, 36, 44, 44) sts for each sleeve; yoke measures about 1½ (1¾, 2, 2¼, 2½)" (3.8 [4.5, 5, 5.5, 6.5] cm) from joining Rnd 1.

20 (21½, 21¾, 22¾, 22¾)"
51 (54.5, 55, 58, 58) cm

4¼ (5¼, 5¾, 6½, 6¾)"
11.5 (13.5, 14.5, 16.5, 17) cm

2 (2¾, 3¼, 3¾, 4¼)"
5 (7, 8.5, 9.5, 11) cm

10¾ (13½, 13½, 16, 16)"
27.5 (34.5, 34.5, 40.5, 40.5) cm

36½ (39, 41¾, 44¼, 46¾)"
92.5 (99, 106, 112.5, 118.5) cm

21 (22, 24, 25, 27)"
53.5 (56, 61, 63.5, 68.5) cm

Front & Back

41 (43¾, 46¾, 49½, 52½)"
104 (111, 118.5, 125.5, 133.5) cm

Work short-rows to shape cap sleeves as foll, turning at the end of each short-row without wrapping any sts at the turning points:

SHORT-ROW 1: (RS) Knit to 2 sts before left front raglan m (second m of rnd), turn.

SHORT-ROW 2: (WS) Yo, purl to 2 sts before left back raglan m (first m of rnd), turn.

SHORT-ROW 3: Yo, knit to 2 sts before previous turning point, turn.

SHORT-ROW 4: Yo, purl to 2 sts before previous turning point, turn.

SHORT-ROWS 5 AND 6: Rep Short-rows 3 and 4 once more.

SHORT-ROW 7: Yo, knit to end of left sleeve sts, knitting each yo tog with the st after it as k2tog, knit across front sts, knit to 2 sts before right back raglan m (4th m of rnd), turn.

SHORT-ROW 8: (WS) Yo, purl to 2 sts before right front raglan m (3rd m of rnd), turn.

SHORT-ROW 9: Yo, knit to 2 sts before previous turning point, turn.

SHORT-ROW 10: Yo, purl to 2 sts before previous turning point, turn.

SHORT-ROWS 11 AND 12: Rep Short-rows 9 and 10 once more.

SHORT-ROW 13: Yo, knit to end of rnd, knitting each yo tog with the st after it as k2tog.

NEXT RND: *Working each rem yo tog with st after it as k2tog, knit to marker, sl m, p2togtbl, knit to 2 sts before next m, p2tog, sl m; rep from * once more, knit to end—2 sts dec'd from each sleeve.

Rep the last rnd 0 (2, 3, 6, 6) more times—140 (151, 152, 159, 160) sts; 22 (22, 24, 24, 25) sts each for left and right back; 46 (47, 48, 51, 50) front sts; 25 (30, 28, 30, 30) sts each sleeve.

NEXT RND: (eyelet rnd) Change to size 10 (6 mm) needle. Work *p2tog, yo; rep from * to last 0 (1, 0, 1, 0) sts, end k0 (1, 0, 1, 0); yoke measures about 2 (2$\frac{3}{4}$, 3$\frac{1}{4}$, 3$\frac{3}{4}$, 4$\frac{1}{4}$)" (5 [7, 8.5, 9.5, 11] cm) above last lace rnd at center front and back and 3 (3$\frac{3}{4}$, 4$\frac{1}{4}$, 5, 5$\frac{1}{4}$)" (7.5 [9.5, 11.5, 12.5, 13.5] cm) above last lace rnd, measured straight up in center of each sleeve.

Using the decrease method (see Glossary), BO all sts.

Finishing

Weave in loose ends. Block to measurements. Use cast-on tails threaded on a tapestry needle to smooth the joins at start of the first sleeve and body rnds. With yarn threaded on a tapestry needle, use the Kitchener st (see Glossary) to graft held sleeve and body sts together at underarms. Weave in loose ends. Beg and end at the left front raglan, thread ribbon in and out of eyelets around neck opening, draw up ribbon to where desired fit is achieved, and tie ends in a bow.

LOUISA

BOTTOM-UP SEAMLESS SET-IN SLEEVE CONSTRUCTION

Elizabeth Zimmermann's *Knitting Workshop* provides basic guidelines for constructing set-in sleeve garments seamlessly from the bottom up. This method is similar to the bottom-up seamless raglan method (see page 90) and will be familiar to knitters who've used the more conventional method of constructing garments from the bottom up in pieces. For the *French Girl Knits* designs, I've modified Elizabeth Zimmermann's original idea to eliminate the large number of stitches that result from joining the body and sleeves. The challenges of the bottom-up seamless set-in sleeve method are—especially for garments with wide necklines—to eliminate enough stitches for a close fit and to provide enough shape in the sleeve cap before completing the upper part of the yoke (where the garment grows over the shoulder). For this type of construction, you can work the sleeves (as for Louisa on page 128) or the body first.

Sleeve-First Method

To work a pullover following this method, work the sleeves in the round to the armholes, then place a few stitches on holders at the underarms (Figure 1). Set the sleeves aside. Cast on stitches for the entire body circumference and work in rounds to the base of the armholes, then place the same number of stitches on holders for each underarm (Figure 2). To join the pieces, use a long circular needle to work the left sleeve stitches, place a marker, work across the front stitches, place another marker, work across the right sleeve stitches, place a marker, work across the back stitches, place a marker, and join for working in rounds (Figure 3). The round begins at the back left shoulder. Work to the neck, decreasing equally at the boundaries between the front, back, and sleeves on every round for a couple of inches. Then decrease on just the sleeves while working short-rows to shape the caps and back neck (Figure 4). You work a cardigan similarly, but back and forth in rows, beginning and ending at the center front.

Body-First Method

Although I didn't use this method for any of the garments in this book, the technique holds promise. In a reverse iteration of the separate body and sleeves version of the top-down seamless set-in sleeve method (see page 106), you work the body in a single piece from the hem to the armholes, then work the front and back separately to the shoulders, shaping the armscye along the way. You join the shoulders by grafting, then pick up stitches around the armholes and work the sleeves in rounds to the cuffs. You work short-rows along the way to shape the caps. A garment with a higher neckline would benefit from this method as well, allowing for a more fitted yoke than Elizabeth Zimmermann outlines.

TIPS FOR BOTTOM-UP SEAMLESS SET-IN SLEEVE CONSTRUCTION

- Reduce the needle size and incorporate ribbed stitch patterns to help shape the upper yoke.

- Existing made-in-pieces patterns, especially those with non-intricate upper bodices, are ideal candidates for exploring this technique.

- If you want to use the method of working the body first, but you want matching design elements at the body hemline (which is worked from the bottom up) and the sleeve cuffs (which would be worked from the top down), consider working the sleeves from the top down to just above the cuff. Place the stitches on a holder, cast on new stitches for the cuffs, and work them from the bottom up. Then graft the two parts together.

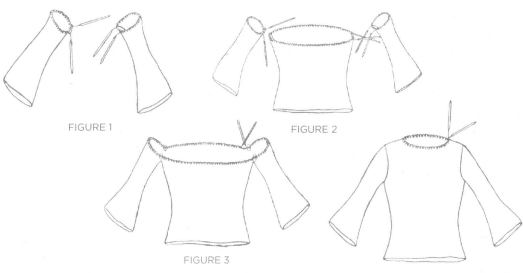

FIGURE 1

FIGURE 2

FIGURE 3

FIGURE 4

VÉRONIQUE * *airy shrug*

FINISHED SIZE

30¾ (34, 37¼, 40¼, 43½, 46½)" (78 [86.5, 94.5, 102, 110.5, 118] cm) bust circumference; fronts do not meet in the middle. Shrug shown measures 30¾" (78 cm). NOTE: This garment may be worn with a narrower or wider gap at center front to accommodate smaller, larger, or in-between sizes.

YARN

Sportweight (#2 Fine).

SHOWN HERE: Rowan Kidsilk Haze (70% kid mohair, 30% silk; 227 yd [208 ml]/25 g): #639 anthracite (dark gray), 3 (3, 4, 4, 4, 5) balls.

NEEDLES

BODY AND SLEEVES: size U.S. 8 (5 mm): 36" (90 cm) circular (cir) and set of 4 or 5 double-pointed (dpn). DECORATIVE BIND-OFF: sizes U.S. 10½ and 11 (6.5 and 8 mm): 36" (90 cm) cir. *Adjust needle size if necessary to obtain the correct gauge.*

NOTIONS

Marker (m); safety pins; waste yarn; tapestry needle.

GAUGE

15 stitches and 22 rows/rounds = 4" (10 cm) in stockinette stitch on size 8 (5 mm) needles.

With Véronique, I sought to put together the most minimal of garments to conjure up a little nighttime mystery for an evening's adventures dans la rue.

The yarn itself, a shade of inky anthracite, evokes a certain phantom quality that seems perfect for a design of this name. As cinema devotees will recall, *La Double Vie de Véronique* (The Double Life of Véronique), Krzysztof Kieślowski's shape-shifting gem of a film, has the circles of two women's lives (one French, the other Polish) folding over, one on the other.

Similarly, this design comes together in a seemingly amorphous way. The body (see Notes) is constructed at an airy gauge to encourage maximum fluidity. The gathered lower back joins the upper portion, leaving openings for the sleeves, which are then worked downward to the desired length. A miniscule bit of lace touches the bind-off. For that extra *soupçon* of *femme fatale* glamour, finish off the hem by adding petite jet or crystal beads.

Notes

- The body is worked in a T shape, beginning at the lower back. After completing the back "skirt" section, the lower back stitches are gathered into the upper back using k3tog decreases.
- Stitches are cast on provisionally at each side of the decreased lower back "skirt" stitches for the top crossbar of the T shape. The crossbar section is worked even to form the upper back and fronts.
- The selvedges of the upper body are sewn to the selvedges of the lower back skirt, leaving the provisional cast-on stitches free for the armholes; the adventurous knitter could work the design completely seamlessly.
- The sleeves are worked in the round from the armholes to lower edges. The sleeves are not shown on the body schematic.
- An optional decorative bind-off creates a flexible, slightly ruffled edge around the entire body.

Body

LOWER BACK

With size 8 (5 mm) cir needle and using a provisional method (see Glossary), CO 111 (135, 159, 183, 207, 231) sts. Do not join. Work back and forth in rows in St st until piece measures 10½ (11, 11½, 12, 12½, 13)" (26.5 [28, 29, 30.5, 31.5, 33] cm) from beg, ending with a WS row.

UPPER BACK AND FRONTS

(RS) Use a provisional method to CO 48 (50, 54, 56, 60, 66) sts at beg of row, knit across new CO sts, [k3tog] 37 (45, 53, 61, 69, 77) times across lower back "skirt" sts, use a provisional method to CO 48 (50, 54, 56, 60, 66) sts at end of row, knit across new CO sts—133 (145, 161, 173, 189, 209) sts total. Work even in St st until piece measures 10½ (11, 11½, 12, 12½, 13)" (26.5 [28, 29, 30.5, 31.5, 33] cm) from where sts were CO at each side. Place all sts on waste yarn.

Sleeves

Block body to finished measurements, taking care not to flatten gathers across top of back skirt. Pin selvedges of upper body to selvedges of lower back at each side, matching corners as shown on assembly diagram; provisional CO sts at each side of upper body rem unattached and will form the armholes. With yarn threaded on a tapestry needle, sew each seam from base of armhole to lower edge. Carefully remove waste yarn from provisional CO at underarm and place 48 (50, 54, 56, 60, 66) exposed sts on size 8 (5 mm) dpn. Place marker (pm) and join for working in rnds. Work even in St st until sleeve measures 12" (30.5 cm) from beg or desired length; sleeve should reach to just below wearer's elbow. Try on garment to check sleeve length and adjust length by adding or removing rnds if necessary. BO all sts loosely.

ASSEMBLY DIAGRAM

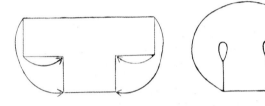

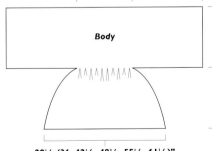

9³/₄ (12, 14, 16¹/₄, 18¹/₂, 20¹/₂)"
25 (30.5, 35.5 41.5, 47, 52) cm

12³/₄ (13¹/₄, 14¹/₂, 15, 16, 17¹/₂)"
32.5 (33.5, 37, 38, 40.5, 44.5) cm

Body

10¹/₂ (11, 11¹/₂, 12, 12¹/₂, 13)"
26.5 (28, 29, 30.5, 31.5, 33) cm

10¹/₂ (11, 11¹/₂, 12, 12¹/₂, 13)"
26.5 (28, 29, 30.5, 31.5, 33) cm

29¹/₂ (36, 42¹/₂, 48³/₄, 55¹/₄, 61¹/₂)"
75 (91.5, 108, 124, 140.5, 156) cm

Finishing

CUSTOMIZING LENGTH

Try shrug on to check body length. The edge with the held sts should fit high against the back neck and curve down along each front, bolero-fashion. The gathers across the top of the lower back skirt should run across the shoulder blades, with the provisional CO edge of the lower back skirt creating a swing effect. With RS facing, carefully place 133 (145, 161, 173, 189, 209) held neck/front edge sts and 111 (135, 159, 183, 207, 231) provisional CO sts of lower back on size 8 (5 mm) cir needle and rejoin yarn to beg of lower back sts—244 (280, 320, 356, 396, 440) sts. Pm and join for working in rnds. If not adding length, skip to Binding Off directions below. If adding length, work St st in rnds as desired; every 5 rnds added will increase the height of the back neck, width of each front, and length of lower back by about 1" (2.5 cm).

BINDING OFF

Change to size 10¹/₂ (6.5 mm) cir needle. Knit 1 rnd, inc 1 st at each end of rnd—246 (282, 322, 358, 398, 442) sts. For a plain, non-ruffled edge, BO all sts using the sewn bind-off method (see Glossary). For a decorative ruffled edge, cont as foll: Change to size 11 (8 mm) cir needle. Keeping a light, loose tension: K2tog, *yo, k1, sl 3 sts back to left needle and knit these 3 sts tog tbl, sl resulting st back to left needle and knit this st tog with the next st; rep from * to end. NOTE: To make working k3togtbl easier, gently pull down on the sts as you insert the right needle tip through their back loops, making sure to catch all 3 sts.

Weave in loose ends.

BIJOU ✳ *cropped cotton cardigan*

"In France they kiss on Main Street. Amour, mama, not cheap display." So sang Joni Mitchell, and so it remains in Paris. In a town far from that City of Love, a peridot-green bijou of a ring caught one young woman's eye. She wished that someday it would be hers, but she returned to find it sold. Unbeknownst to her (and after several clandestine maneuvers later), this jewel waited in the safe of the Paris hotel where she and her beloved would spend their winter holiday. The dear man who performed this sleight of hand was prepared to profess his affection on bended knee at any turn should the ring be discovered before the perfect moment arrived . . . and arrive it did.

Across the Seine, Pont de Solférino was white with falling snow on that first day of the new year as he reached for the ring she had coveted and thought lost. In that moment, she thought it might be lost again, tumbling into the river's current, their hands were shaking so. But as all good stories, this story ends well. Although I can't promise you a marriage proposal in Paris if you knit Bijou, I know you'll have a garment as lighthearted and as easy to wear as young love.

FINISHED SIZE

34 (38, 42, 45, 49)" (86.5 [96.5, 106.5, 114.5, 124.5] cm) bust circumference, including width of both 1½" (3.8 cm) seed-stitch bands at center front. Sweater shown measures 34" (86.5 cm).

YARN

Worsted weight (#4 Medium).

SHOWN HERE: Blue Sky Alpacas Dyed Cotton (100% organic cotton; 150 yd [137 ml/100 g]): #634 periwinkle (A), 3 (4, 4, 5, 5) balls.

Blue Sky Alpacas Organic Cotton (100% organic cotton; 150 yd [137 ml/100 g]): #80 bone (natural, B), 3 (3, 3, 4, 4) balls.

NEEDLES

BODY AND SLEEVES: size U.S. 7 (4.5 mm): 16" and 40" (40 and 100 cm) circular (cir) and set of 4 or 5 double-pointed (dpn). CAST-ON: sizes U.S. 5 and 6 (3.75 and 4 mm): straight. EDGING: size U.S. 4 (3.5 mm): 40" (100 cm) cir. *Adjust needle size if necessary to obtain the correct gauge.*

NOTIONS

Marker (m); removable markers; stitch holders; wooden buckle with 2" (5 cm) center post; smooth cotton waste yarn for provisional cast-on; size H/8 (4.75 mm) crochet hook; tapestry needle.

GAUGE

17½ stitches and 30 rows/rounds = 4" (10 cm) in beaded-stitch pattern on largest needles.

Notes

The garment is worked in two halves, each half beginning at the sleeve cuff and worked in the round to the top of the sleeve where stitches are provisionally cast on at each side for the back and front. Work continues back and forth in rows to the neck edge where the front stitches are placed on a holder. The back stitches are worked separately to center back, then the front stitches are returned to the needle and worked to center front. The two pieces are grafted together at center back.

The schematic does not show the edging, which will add about 1½" (3.8 cm) to the length of the lower body after finishing.

Stitch Guide

PRB
Purl into st in the row below the next st on left needle—1 st inc'd.

KRB
Knit into st in the row below the next st on left needle—1 st inc'd.

BEADED STRIPE PATTERN IN ROUNDS
(MULTIPLE OF 6 STS)
RND 1: (RS) With A, knit.
RND 2: (WS) With A, *k3, p3; rep from *.
RND 3: With B, *sl 3 pwise with yarn in back (wyb), k3; rep from *.
RND 4: With B, k1, *sl 1 pwise wyb, k5; rep from * to last 5 sts, sl 1 pwise wyb, k4.
RND 5: With B, knit.
RND 6: With B, *p3, k3; rep from *.
RND 7: With A, *k3, sl 3 pwise wyb; rep from *.
RND 8: With A, k4,*sl 1 wyb, k5; rep from * to last 2 sts, sl 1 wyb, k1.
Repeat Rnds 1–8 for pattern.

BEADED STRIPE PATTERN IN ROWS
(MULTIPLE OF 6 STS + 5)
ROW 1: (RS) With A, knit.
ROW 2: (WS) With A, k1, *p3, k3; rep from * to last 4 sts, p3, k1.
ROW 3: With B, k1, *sl 3 pwise wyb, k3; rep from * to last 4 sts, sl 3 pwise wyb, k1.
ROW 4: With B, k1, p1, *sl 1 pwise with yarn in front (wyf), p5; rep from * to last 3 sts, sl 1 pwise wyf, p1, k1.
ROW 5: With B, knit.
ROW 6: With B, k4, *p3, k3; rep from * to last st, k1.
ROW 7: With A, k4, *sl 3 pwise wyb, k3; rep from * to last st, k1.
ROW 8: With A, k1, p4, *sl 1 pwise wyf, p5; rep from * to last 6 sts, sl 1 pwise wyf, p4, k1.
Repeat Rows 1–8 for pattern. NOTE: Do not cut yarns between rnds; instead, carry the unused yarn along the WS of the fabric until it is needed again, twisting both yarns around each after completing every rnd.

SEED STITCH (EVEN NUMBER OF STS)
RND 1: *K1, p1; rep from *.
RND 2: Purl the knit sts, and knit the purl sts as they appear.
Rep Rnd 2 for pattern.

MITERED CORNER INCREASE
Work in patt to marked corner st, work krb or prb as required to maintain seed st patt, knit the corner st, work krb or prb to maintain seed st patt in next st, work next st in patt—2 sts inc'd, 1 on each side of marked corner st.

MITERED CORNER DECREASE
Work in patt to 2 sts before marked corner st, work next 2 sts tog as k2tog or p2tog to maintain seed st patt, knit the corner st, work next 2 sts tog as k2tog or p2tog to maintain patt—2 sts dec'd, 1 on each side of marked corner st.

Right Half

SLEEVE

With A, size 6 (4 mm) straight needles, and using the cable method (see Glossary), CO 48 (54, 60, 66, 72) sts. Knit 1 RS row. Change to size 7 (4.5 mm) dpn. Place marker (pm) and join for working in rnds, being careful not to twist sts. Work Rnds 1–8 of beaded stripe patt in rnds (see Stitch Guide) 4 (4, 4, 5, 5) times, then work Rnd 1 once more—33 (33, 33, 41, 41) patt rnds completed; piece measures about 4½ (4½, 4½, 5½, 5½)" (11.5 [11.5, 11.5, 14, 14] cm) from CO.

INC RND: Inc 1 in first st using either krb or prb (see Stitch Guide) as needed to maintain patt, work in patt to last st, inc 1 in last st using either krb or prb, work last st—2 sts inc'd.

Work inc rnd on next rnd, then work 1 rnd even, work inc rnd on next 2 rnds, work 1 rnd even, working new sts into patt, and ending with Rnd 7 of patt—56 (62, 68, 74, 80) sts. [Work inc rnd on next 3 rnds, work 2 rnds even] 3 times, changing to size 7 (4.5 mm) 16" (40 cm) cir needle when there are too many sts to fit on dpn and ending with Rnd 6 of patt—74 (80, 86, 92, 98) sts; 54 (54, 54, 62, 62) patt rnds completed. Work next 0 (1, 1, 0, 0) rnd, inc 2 sts as for inc rnd—74 (82, 88, 92, 98) sts.

NEXT RND: Work in patt to last st, inc 1 st in last st using either krb or prb, work last st—75 (83, 89, 93, 99) sts.

Work 1 (0, 0, 1, 1) rnd even, ending with Rnd 8 of patt—piece measures about 7½ (7½, 7½, 8½, 8½)" (19 [19, 19, 21.5, 21.5] cm) from CO.

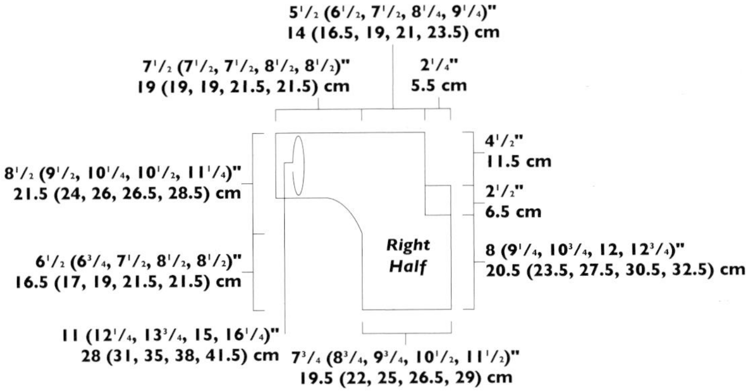

FRONT AND BACK

With crochet hook, smooth waste yarn, and using the crochet-on method (see Glossary), provisionally CO 29 (31, 34, 38, 38) right front sts onto size 6 (4 mm) straight needle. Join new ball of A to beg of CO sts with RS facing. With size 7 (4.5 mm) longer cir needle, work Row 1 of beaded stripe patt in rows (see Stitch Guide) to last new CO st, work next 2 sts (last CO st and first sleeve st) tog as k2tog or p2tog to maintain patt, cont in established patt to last sleeve st, set aside temporarily. With size 5 (4 mm) straight needle and working from lower edge to underarm, pick up and knit 29 (31, 34, 38, 38) sts for right back from main yarn loops at base of front provisional CO sts. With RS facing and yarn attached to end of sleeve, work next 2 sts (last sleeve st and first CO st) tog as k2tog or p2tog to maintain patt, work in patt to end—131 (143, 155, 167, 173) sts total. NOTE: Because there are sts worked from both sides of the same

5½ (6½, 7½, 8¼, 9¼)"
14 (16.5, 19, 21, 23.5) cm

7½ (7½, 7½, 8½, 8½)"
19 (19, 19, 21.5, 21.5) cm

2¼"
5.5 cm

8½ (9½, 10¼, 10½, 11¼)"
21.5 (24, 26, 26.5, 28.5) cm

4½"
11.5 cm

2½"
6.5 cm

Right Half

6½ (6¾, 7½, 8½, 8½)"
16.5 (17, 19, 21.5, 21.5) cm

8 (9¼, 10¾, 12, 12¾)"
20.5 (23.5, 27.5, 30.5, 32.5) cm

11 (12¼, 13¾, 15, 16¼)"
28 (31, 35, 38, 41.5) cm

7¾ (8¾, 9¾, 10½, 11½)"
19.5 (22, 25, 26.5, 29) cm

provisional CO, the cable section of the cir needle will be folded in half in a tight hairpin bend; it will become easier to slide the sts around this bend as the work progresses. Work Rows 2–8 of patt once, rep Rows 1–8 of patt 4 (5, 6, 6, 7) more times, then work Rows 1–4 of patt 0 (0, 0, 1, 1) time, then work Row 1 (1, 1, 5, 5) once more—piece measures about 5½ (6½, 7½, 8¼, 9¼)" (14 [16.5, 19, 21, 23.5] cm) from front and back CO and about 13 (14, 15, 16¾, 17¾)" (33 [35.5, 38, 42.5, 45] cm) from beg of sleeve.

Right Back

(WS) Work 46 (52, 58, 64, 67) back sts in patt, place rem 85 (91, 97, 103, 106) sts on holder for right back neck and right front. Cont in established patt on right back sts for 15 more rows, ending with Row 1 (1, 1, 5, 5) of patt—piece measures about 2¼" (5.5 cm) from where back neck and front sts were put on holder, 7¾ (8¾, 9¾, 10½, 11½)" (19.5 [22, 25, 26.5, 29] cm) from sts CO for side of lower body, and about 15¼ (16¼, 17¼, 19, 20)" (38.5 [41.5, 44, 48.5, 51] cm) from beg of sleeve. Place sts on holder.

Right Front

With RS facing, place first 35 (41, 47, 53, 56) held sts on size 7 (4.5 cm) longer cir needle, leaving rem 50 sts on holder for back and front neck. Rejoin yarn in color for Row 2 (2, 2, 6, 6) with WS facing. Beg with WS Row 2 (2, 2, 6, 6), work 16 rows in established patt, ending with Row 1 (1, 1, 5, 5)—piece measures same length as right back. Place sts on holder.

Left Half

SLEEVE

Work as for right half—75 (83, 89, 93, 99) sts; piece measures about 7½ (7½, 7½, 8½, 8½)" (19 [19, 19, 21.5, 21.5] cm) from CO.

FRONT AND BACK

With crochet hook, smooth waste yarn, and using the crochet-on method, CO 29 (31, 34, 38, 38) left back sts onto size 6 (4 mm) straight needle. Join new ball of A to beg of CO sts with RS facing. With size 7 (4.5 cm) longer cir needle, work Row 1 of beaded stripe patt in rows to last new CO st, work next 2 sts (last CO st and first sleeve st) tog as k2tog or p2tog to maintain patt, cont in established patt to last sleeve st, set aside temporarily. With size 5 (4 mm) straight needle and working from lower edge to underarm, pick up and knit 29 (31, 34, 38, 38) sts for left front from main yarn loops at base of provisional CO sts. With RS facing and yarn attached to end of sleeve, work next 2 sts (last sleeve st and first CO st) tog as k2tog or p2tog to maintain

patt, work in patt to end—131 (143, 155, 167, 173) sts total. Work Rows 2–8 once, rep Rows 1–8 of patt 4 (5, 6, 6, 7) more times, work Rows 1–4 of patt 0 (0, 0, 1, 1) time, then work Row 1 (1, 1, 5, 5) once more—piece measures about 5½ (6½, 7½, 8¼, 9¼)" (14 [16.5, 19, 21, 23.5] cm) from front and back CO and about 13 (14, 15, 16¾, 17¾)" (33 [35.5, 38, 42.5, 45] cm) from beg of sleeve.

Left Front

(WS) Work 35 (41, 47, 53, 56) left front sts in patt, place rem 96 (102, 108, 114, 117) sts on holder for left front neck and back. Cont in established patt on left front sts for 15 more rows, ending with Row 1 (1, 1, 5, 5) of patt—piece measures about 2¼" (5.5 cm) from where back neck and front sts were put on holder, 7¾ (8¾, 9¾, 10½, 11½)" (19.5 [22, 25, 26.5, 29] cm) from sts CO for side of lower body, and about 15¼ (16¼, 17¼, 19, 20)" (38.5 [41.5, 44, 48.5, 51] cm) from beg of sleeve. Place sts on holder.

Left Back

With RS facing, place first 46 (52, 58, 64, 67) held sts on size 7 (4.5 cm) longer cir needle, leaving rem 50 sts on holder for back and front neck. Rejoin yarn in color for Row 2 (2, 2, 6, 6) with WS facing. Beg with WS Row 2 (2, 2, 6, 6), work 16 rows in established patt, ending with Row 1 (1, 1, 5, 5)—piece measures same length as left front. Place sts on holder.

Finishing

Block to finished measurements. With yarn threaded on a tapestry needle, use the Kitchener st (see Glossary) to graft the 46 (52, 58, 64, 67) sts of the right and left backs tog.

EDGING

With A, size 4 (3.5 mm) cir needle, RS facing, and beg in center of lower back edge, pick up and knit 28 (32, 35, 38, 42) sts to base of right side "seam," then 28 (32, 35, 38, 42) sts from "seam" to lower right front corner, pick up 1 st in lower right front corner and hang a removable marker (m) in the corner st itself (not on needle between sts), k35 (41, 47, 53, 56) held right front sts, pick up and knit 1 st in top right front corner and hang removable m in this st, pick up and knit 9 sts along right front selvedge to right front neck corner, pick up and knit 1 st in neck corner and hang removable m in this st, k50 held sts from right side of neck, pick up and knit 1 st in right back neck corner and hang removable m in this st, pick up and knit 20 sts across back neck, pick up and knit 1 st in left back neck corner and hang removable m in this st, k50 held sts from left side of neck, pick up and knit 1 st in left front neck corner and hang a removable m in this st, pick up and knit 9 sts along left front selvedge to top left corner, pick up and knit 1 st in corner and hang removable m in this st, k35 (41, 47, 53, 56) held left front sts, pick up and knit 1 st in lower left front corner and hang removable m in this st, pick up and knit 28 (32, 35, 38, 42) sts across lower edge of left front to base of left side "seam," then 28 (32, 35, 38, 42) sts across lower edge of back to center back—328 (356, 380, 404, 426) sts total. Place regular m on needle and join for working in rnds. Work seed st with mitered corners as foll:

RND 1: Work Rnd 1 of seed st (see Stitch Guide).

RND 2: Work seed st as established to marked lower right front corner st, work mitered corner inc (see Stitch Guide), work in patt to marked upper right front corner st, work mitered corner inc, work in patt to 2 sts before marked right front neck corner st, work mitered corner dec (see Stitch Guide), work in patt to 2 sts before marked right back neck corner st, work mitered corner dec, work in patt to 2 sts before marked left back neck corner st, work mitered corner dec, work in patt to 2 sts before marked left front neck corner st, work mitered corner dec, work in patt to upper left front corner st, work mitered corner inc, work in patt to lower left front corner st, work mitered corner inc, work in patt to end—no change in st count; 2 sts dec'd at each of 4 neck corner sts; 2 sts inc'd at each of 4 front corner sts.

RND 3: Work even in patt, knitting all marked corner sts.

RNDS 4–10: Rep Rnds 2 and 3 three more times, then work Rnd 2 once more—edging measures about 1½" (3.8 cm) from pick-up rnd.

BO all sts in seed-st patt on next rnd.

TAB AND BUCKLE

With A, size 4 (3.5 cm) needle, RS facing, and beg 13 sts down from upper right front corner, pick up and knit 13 sts along BO edge of right front to end at corner.

NEXT ROW: [K1, p1] 6 times, k1.

Rep the last row 23 more times—tab measures about 3¼" (8.5 cm) from pick-up row. BO all sts in seed st patt. With A threaded on a tapestry needle, sew center post of buckle to BO edge of left front, opposite tab.

Weave in loose ends.

glossary

ABBREVIATIONS

beg	begin(s); beginning		rep	repeat(s); repeating
BO	bind off		rev St st	reverse stockinette stitch
CC	contrast color		rnd(s)	round(s)
cm	centimeter(s)		RS	right side
cn	cable needle		sl	slip
CO	cast on		sl st	slip st (slip 1 stitch purlwise unless otherwise indicated)
cont	continue(s); continuing			
dec(s)	decrease(s); decreasing		ssk	slip 2 stitches knitwise, one at a time, from the left needle to right needle, insert left needle tip through both front loops and knit together from this position (1 stitch decrease)
dpn	double-pointed needles			
foll	follow(s); following			
g	gram(s)			
inc(s)	increase(s); increasing			
k	knit		st	stitch(es)
k1f&b	knit into the front and back of same stitch		St st	stockinette stitch
			tbl	through back loop
kwise	knitwise, as if to knit		tog	together
m	marker(s)		WS	wrong side
MC	main color		wyb	with yarn in back
mm	millimeter(s)		wyf	with yarn in front
M1	make one (increase)		yd	yard(s)
p	purl		yo	yarnover
p1f&b	purl into front and back of same stitch		*	repeat starting point
			* *	repeat all instructions between asterisks
patt(s)	pattern(s)			
psso	pass slipped stitch over		( )	alternate measurements and/or instructions
pwise	purlwise, as if to purl			
rem	remain(s); remaining		[ ]	work instructions as a group a specified number of times

Sewn Bind-Off

Cut yarn three times the width of the knitting to be bound off, then thread onto a tapestry needle. Working from right to left, *insert tapestry needle purlwise (from right to left) through the first two stitches (Figure 1) and pull the yarn through. Bring tapestry needle knitwise (from left to right) through first stitch (Figure 2), pull yarn through, and slip this stitch off the knitting needle. Repeat from * for desired number of stitches.

Decrease Bind-Off

Using a larger needle or working very loosely to prevent bind-off edge from becoming too tight, *k2tog (Figure 1), slip this stitch onto the left needle tip without twisting it (Figure 2). Repeat from *.

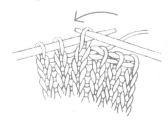

FIGURE 1

FIGURE 2

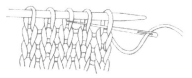

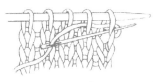

FIGURE 1

FIGURE 2

BLOCKING

Steam-Blocking

Pin the pieces to be blocked to a flat, steam-proof surface. Hold an iron set on the steam setting 1/2" (1.5 cm) above the knitted surface and direct the steam over the entire surface (except ribbing). You can get similar results by lapping wet cheesecloth on top of the knitted surface and touching it lightly with a dry iron. Lift and set down the iron gently; do not use a pushing motion.

Wet-Blocking

Fill a basin with lukewarm water and add a bit of fabric conditioner. Place the knitted piece in the basin, gently squeeze the water through it with as little agitation as possible, then allow it to soak for 20 minutes or more. Squeeze out the water, then roll the piece in a large bath or beach towel to remove excess moisture. Pin the damp piece to a blocking surface and let air-dry thoroughly.

Backward-Loop Cast-On

*Loop working yarn and place it on needle backward so that it doesn't unwind. Repeat from *.

Cable Cast-On

If there are no stitches on the needles, make a slipknot of working yarn and place it on the needle, then use the knitted method to cast-on one more stitch—two stitches on needle. Hold needle with working yarn in your left hand with the wrong side of the work facing you. *Insert right needle between the first two stitches on left needle (Figure 1), wrap yarn around needle as if to knit, draw yarn through (Figure 2), and place new loop on left needle (Figure 3) to form a new stitch. Repeat from * for the desired number of stitches, always working between the first two stitches on the left needle.

FIGURE 1   FIGURE 2   FIGURE 3

Crochet-On Provisional Cast-On

Place a slipknot on a crochet hook. Hold the needle and yarn in your left hand with the yarn under the needle. Place hook over needle, wrap yarn around hook, and pull the loop through the slipknot (Figure 1). *Bring yarn to back under needle, wrap yarn around hook, and pull it through loop on hook (Figure 2). Repeat from * until there is one less than desired number of stitches. Bring the yarn to the back and slip the remaining loop from the hook onto the needle.

FIGURE 1   FIGURE 2

Invisible Provisional Cast-On

Make a loose slipknot of working yarn and place it on the right needle. Hold a length of contrasting waste yarn next to the slipknot and around your left thumb; hold working yarn over your left index finger. *Bring the right needle forward, then under waste yarn, over working yarn, grab a loop of working yarn and bring it forward under working yarn (Figure 1), then bring needle back behind the working yarn and grab a second loop (Figure 2). Repeat from * for the desired number of stitches. When you're ready to work in the opposite direction, place the exposed loops on a knitting needle as you pull out the waste yarn.

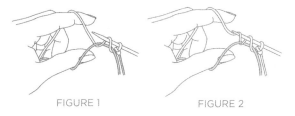

FIGURE 1   FIGURE 2

Knitted Cast-On

Make a slipknot of working yarn and place it on the left needle if there are no stitches already there. *Use the right needle to knit the first stitch (or slipknot) on left needle (Figure 1) and place new loop onto left needle to form a new stitch (Figure 2). Repeat from * for the desired number of stitches, always working into the last stitch made.

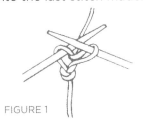
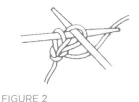

FIGURE 1   FIGURE 2

Long-Tail (Continental) Cast-On

Leaving a long tail (about ½" [1.3 cm] for each stitch to be cast on), make a slipknot and place on right needle. Place thumb and index finger of your left hand between the yarn ends so that working yarn is around your index finger and tail end is around your thumb and secure the yarn ends with your other fingers. Hold your palm upwards, making a V of yarn (Figure 1). *Bring needle up through loop on thumb (Figure 2), catch first strand around index finger, and go back down through loop on thumb (Figure 3). Drop loop off thumb and, placing thumb back in V configuration, tighten resulting stitch on needle (Figure 4). Repeat from * for the desired number of stitches.

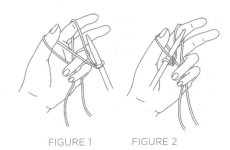

FIGURE 1   FIGURE 2

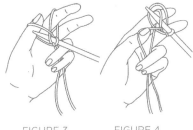

FIGURE 3   FIGURE 4

CROCHET

Crochet Chain (ch)

Make a slipknot and place it on crochet hook if there isn't a loop already on the hook. *Yarn over hook and draw through loop on hook. Repeat from * for the desired number of stitches. To fasten off, cut yarn and draw end through last loop formed.

Double Crochet (dc)

*Yarn over hook, insert hook into a stitch, yarn over hook and draw a loop through (three loops on hook), yarn over hook (Figure 1) and draw a loop through two loops, yarn over hook and draw it through the remaining two loops (Figure 2). Repeat from * for the desired number of stitches.

FIGURE 1   FIGURE 2

Single Crochet (sc)

*Insert hook into the second chain from the hook (or the next stitch), yarn over hook and draw through a loop, yarn over hook (Figure 1), and draw it through both loops on hook (Figure 2). Repeat from * for the desired number of stitches.

FIGURE 1   FIGURE 2

Slip-Stitch Crochet (sl st)

*Insert hook into stitch, yarn over hook and draw a loop through both the stitch and the loop already on hook. Repeat from * for the desired number of stitches.

DECREASES

Knit Two Together Through Back Loops (k2togtbl)

Knit two stitches together through the loops on the back of the needle.

Knit Three Together Through Back Loops (k3togtbl)

Work as for k2togtbl but knit three stitches together through the loops on the back of the needle.

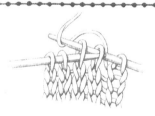

Purl Two Together Through Back Loops (p2togtbl)

Bring right needle tip behind two stitches on left needle, enter through the back loops of the second stitch, then the first stitch, then purl them together.

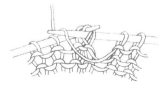

Slip, Slip, Knit (ssk)

Slip two stitches individually knitwise (Figure 1), insert left needle tip into the front of these two slipped stitches, and use the right needle to knit them together through their back loops (Figure 2).

FIGURE 1   FIGURE 2

Slip, Slip, Slip, Knit (sssk)

Slip three stitches individually knitwise (Figure 1), insert left needle tip into the front of these three slipped stitches, and use the right needle to knit them together through their back loops (Figure 2).

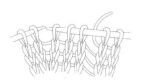 

FIGURE 1   FIGURE 2

Slip, Slip, Purl (ssp)

Holding yarn in front, slip two stitches individually knitwise (Figure 1), then slip these two stitches back onto left needle (they will be turned on the needle) and purl them together through their back loops (Figure 2).

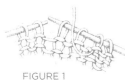 

FIGURE 1   FIGURE 2

EMBROIDERY

Buttonhole Stitch

Working into the edge half-stitch of the knitted piece, *bring tip of threaded needle in and out of a knitted stitch, place working yarn under needle tip, then bring threaded needle through the stitch and tighten. Repeat from *, always bringing threaded needle on top of working yarn.

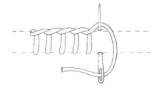

Running Stitch

Bring threaded needle in and out of background to form a dashed line.

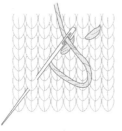

Stem Stitch

Bring threaded needle out of knitted background from back to front at the center of a knitted stitch. *Insert the needle into the upper right edge of the next stitch to the right, then out again at the center of the stitch below. Repeat from * as desired.

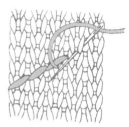

GRAFTING

Kitchener Stitch

Arrange stitches on two needles so that there is the same number of stitches on each needle. Hold the needles parallel to each other with wrong sides of the knitting together. Allowing about 1/2" (1.3 cm) per stitch to be grafted, thread matching yarn on a tapestry needle. Work from right to left as follows:

STEP 1. Bring tapestry needle through the first stitch on the front needle as if to purl and leave the stitch on the needle (Figure 1).

STEP 2. Bring tapestry needle through the first stitch on the back needle as if to knit and leave that stitch on the needle (Figure 2).

STEP 3. Bring tapestry needle through the first front stitch as if to knit and slip this stitch off the needle, then bring tapestry needle through the next front stitch as if to purl and leave this stitch on the needle (Figure 3).

STEP 4. Bring tapestry needle through the first back stitch as if to purl and slip this stitch off the needle, then bring tapestry needle through the next back stitch as if to knit and leave this stitch on the needle (Figure 4).

Repeat Steps 3 and 4 until one stitch remains on each needle, adjusting the tension to match the rest of the knitting as you go. To finish, bring tapestry needle through the front stitch as if to knit and slip this stitch off the needle, then bring tapestry needle through the back stitch as if to purl and slip this stitch off the needle.

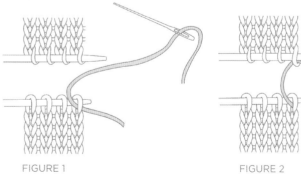

FIGURE 1　　　　　　　　FIGURE 2

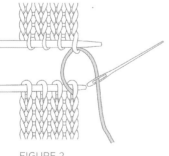

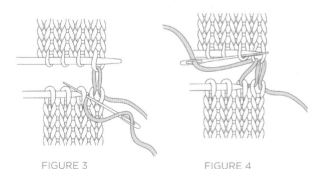

FIGURE 3　　　　　　　　FIGURE 4

Bar Increase (k1f&b)

Knit into a stitch but leave it on the left needle
(Figure 1), then knit through the back loop of the same stitch
(Figure 2) and slip the original stitch off the needle (Figure 3).

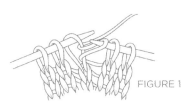

FIGURE 1

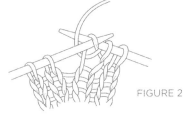

FIGURE 2

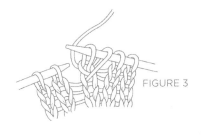

FIGURE 3

Lifted Increase — Left Slant (LLI)

Insert left needle tip into the back of the stitch (in the "purl bump") in the row
directly below the stitch just knitted (Figure 1), then knit this stitch (Figure 2).

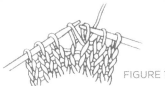

FIGURE 1

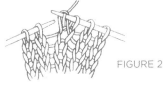

FIGURE 2

Lifted Increase — Right Slant (LRI)

NOTE: If no slant direction is specified, use the right slant.

Knit into the back of the stitch (in the "purl bump") in the row directly below
the next stitch on the needle (Figure 1), then knit the stitch on the needle
(Figure 2), and slip the original stitch off the needle.

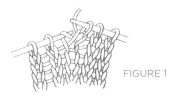

FIGURE 1

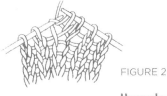

FIGURE 2

Raised Make-One—Left Slant (M1L)

NOTE: Use the left slant if no direction of slant is specified.

With left needle tip, lift the strand between the last knitted stitch and the first stitch on the left needle from front to back (Figure 1), then knit the lifted loop through the back (Figure 2).

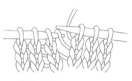

FIGURE 1

FIGURE 2

Raised Make-One—Right Slant (M1R)

With left needle tip, lift the strand between the needles from back to front (Figure 1). Knit the lifted loop through the front (Figure 2).

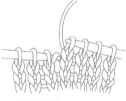

FIGURE 1

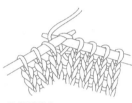

FIGURE 2

Raised Make-One—Purlwise (M1P)

With left needle tip, lift the strand between the needles from front to back (Figure 1), then purl the lifted loop through the back (Figure 2).

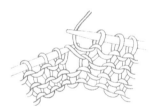

FIGURE 1

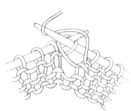

FIGURE 2

Short-rows Knit Side

Work to turning point, slip next stitch purlwise (Figure 1), bring the yarn to the front, then slip the same stitch back to the left needle (Figure 2), turn the work so the purl side is facing and bring the yarn in position for the next stitch—one stitch has been wrapped and the yarn is correctly positioned to work the next stitch. When you come to a wrapped stitch on a subsequent row, hide the wrap by working it together with the wrapped stitch as follows: Insert right needle tip under the wrap (from the front if wrapped stitch is a knit stitch; from the back if wrapped stitch is a purl stitch; Figure 3), then into the stitch on the needle, and work the stitch and its wrap together as a single stitch.

Short-rows Purl Side

Work to the turning point, slip the next stitch purlwise to the right needle, bring the yarn to the back of the work (Figure 1), return the slipped stitch to the left needle, bring the yarn to the front between the needles (Figure 2), and turn the work so that the knit side is facing—one stitch has been wrapped and the yarn is correctly positioned to knit the next stitch. To hide the wrap on a subsequent purl row, work to the wrapped stitch, use the tip of the right needle to pick up the wrap from the back, place it on the left needle (Figure 3), then purl it together with the wrapped stitch.

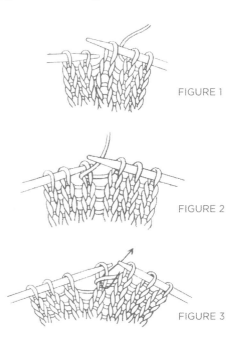

FIGURE 1

FIGURE 2

FIGURE 3

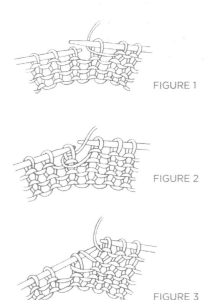

FIGURE 1

FIGURE 2

FIGURE 3

SOURCES FOR SUPPLIES

BEAVERSLIDE DRY GOODS
PO Box 153
Dupuyer, MT 59432
beaverslide.com

BEE SWEET PRODUCTS
1315 Bridgeway
Sausalito, CA 94965
beesweetproducts.com

BLUE SKY ALPACAS INC.
PO Box 88
Cedar, MN 55011
blueskyalpacas.com

**CLASSIC ELITE YARNS /
TWINKLE**
122 Western Ave.
Lowell, MA 01851
classiceliteyarns.com

DIAMOND YARN
9697 St. Laurent, Ste. 101
Montréal, QC
Canada H3L 2N1
and
155 Martin Ross, Unit 3
Toronto, ON
Canada M3J 2L9
diamondyarn.com

**KNITTING FEVER INC. /
LOUISA HARDING /
ELSEBETH LAVOLD**
PO Box 336
315 Bayview Ave.
Amityville, NY 11701
knittingfever.com
In Canada: Diamond Yarn

LOUET NORTH AMERICA
808 Commerce Park Dr.
Ogdensburg, NY 13669
louet.com
In Canada:
3425 Hands Rd.
Prescott, ON K0E 1T0

THE FIBRE COMPANY
c/o Kelbourne Woolens
915 N. 28th St., 2nd Fl.
Philadelphia, PA 19130
thefibreco.com

**VERMONT ORGANIC
FIBER COMPANY**
52 Seymour St., Ste. 8
Middlebury, VT 05753
vtorganicfiber.com

WESTMINSTER FIBERS/ROWAN
165 Ledge St.
Nashua, NH 03060
westminsterfibers.com
In Canada: Diamond Yarn

ONLINE SOURCES

Chicknits.com—adorable, modern, stylish individual patterns, some seamless.

Kinokuniya.com—Japanese knitting patterns and stitch books.

Knitty.com—free diverse, fun patterns and brilliant technical advice.

KnittingDaily.com—*Interweave Knits* online blog; friendly and informative.

Knittinghelp.com—very helpful visual tutorials that demystify and educate.

Knittingpureandsimple.com—basic seamless patterns sold individually.

Ravelry.com—international knit and crochet meet up with literally a world of information and inspiration.

Sweaterbabe.com—girly, mostly seamless individual patterns.

Techknitting.blogspot.com—expansive compendium of techniques.

BIBLIOGRAPHY

Seamless Inspiration and Technique
(IN-DEPTH AND INNOVATIVE PIONEERS)

Fee, Jacqueline. *The Sweater Workshop*. Loveland, Colorado: Interweave, 1983.

Walker, Barbara G. *Knitting from the Top*. Pittsville, Wisconsin: Schoolhouse Press, 1996.

Elizabeth Zimmermann. *Knitting Around*. Pittsville, Wisconsin: Schoolhouse Press, 1989.

__. *Elizabeth Zimmermann's Knitting Workshop*. Pittsville Wisconsin: Schoolhouse Press, 1981.

__. *Knitting Without Tears: Basic Techniques and Easy-to-Follow Directions for Garments to Fit All Sizes*. New York: Simon & Schuster, 1971.

Fresh Faces
(CONTINUING THE SEAMLESS EXPLORATION)

Bernhard, Wendy. *Custom Knits*. New York: Stewart Tabori & Chang, 2008.

Japel, Stefanie. *Fitted Knits: 25 Projects for the Fashionable Knitter*. Cincinnati, Ohio: North Light Books, 2007.

__. *Glam Knits: 25 Designs for Luxe Yarns*. Cincinnati, Ohio: North Light Books, 2008.

Stafford, Jennifer. *DomiKNITrix: Whip Your Knitting into Shape*. Cincinnati, Ohio: North Light Books, 2006.

French Girl Deliciousness
(FEMININE, FLIRTY BOOKS)

Allen, Pam, and Ann Budd. *Lace Style: Traditional to Innovative, 21 Inspired Designs to Knit*. Loveland, Colorado: Interweave, 2007.

Cropper, Susan. *Pretty Knits: 30 Designs from Loop in London*. New York: Potter Craft, 2007.

__. *Vintage Crochet: 30 Gorgeous Designs for Home, Garden, Fashion, Gifts*. New York: Watson-Guptill, 2007.

Harding, Louisa. *Dauphine Pattern Book*. Louisa Harding, 2007.

Hargreaves, Kim. *Heartfelt Pattern Book*. Kim Hargreaves, 2007.

__. *Nectar Pattern Book*. Kim Hargreaves, 2008.

Orne, Michele Rose. *Inspired to Knit: Creating Exquisite Handknits*. Loveland, Colorado: Interweave, 2008.

Knitting Technique & Yarn Research

Budd, Ann. *The Knitter's Handy Book of Sweater Patterns: Basic Designs in Multiple Sizes and Gauges*. Loveland, Colorado: Interweave, 2004.

Parkes, Clara. *The Knitter's Book of Yarn: The Ultimate Guide to Choosing, Using, and Enjoying Yarn*. New York: Potter Craft, 2007.

Radcliffe, Margaret. *The Knitting Answer Book: Solutions to Every Problem You'll Ever Face; Answers to Every Question You'll Ever Ask*. North Adams, Massachusetts: Storey Publishing, 2005.

Singer, Amy R. *No Sheep for You*. Loveland, Colorado: Interweave, 2007.

Stanley, Montse. *Knitter's Handbook: A Comprehensive Guide to the Principles and Techniques of Handknitting*. Reader's Digest, 1999.

Sowerby, Jane, and Alexis Xenakis. *Victorian Lace Today*. Sioux Falls, South Dakota: XRX Books, 2008.

Thomas, Mary. *Mary Thomas's Book of Knitting Patterns.* Mineola, New York: Dover Publications, 1972.

__. *Mary Thomas's Knitting Book.* Mineola, New York: Dover Publications, 1972.

Vogue Knitting Magazine Editors. *Vogue Knitting: The Ultimate Knitting Book.* New York: Sixth and Spring Books, 2002.

Wiseman, Nancie M. *The Knitter's Book of Finishing Techniques.* Woodinville, Washington: Martingale & Company, 2002.

Stitch Dictionaries

Epstein, Nicky. *Knitting on the Edge.* New York: Sixth and Spring Books, 2004.

Nihon Vogue. Check online for a variety of Japanese books of knitting stitch patterns.

Walker, Barbara G. *A Treasury of Knitting Patterns.* Pittsville, Wisconsin: Schoolhouse Press, 1998.

__. *A Second Treasury of Knitting Patterns.* Pittsville, Wisconsin: Schoolhouse Press, 1998.

__. *Charted Knitting Designs: A Third Treasury of Knitting Patterns.* Pittsville, Wisconsin: Schoolhouse Press, 1998.

__. *A Fourth Treasury of Knitting Patterns.* Pittsville, Wisconsin: Schoolhouse Press, 2000.

In a Class by Themselves
(NOT NECESSARILY SEAMLESS, BUT CERTAINLY INSPIRED)

Chan, Doris. *Everyday Crochet: Wearable Designs Just for You.* New York: Potter Craft, 2007.

Durham, Teva. *Loop-d-Loop: More than 40 Novel Designs for Knitters.* New York: Harry N. Abrams, 2005.

__. *Loop-d-Loop Crochet: More than 25 Novel Designs for Crocheters (and Knitters Taking Up the Hook).* New York: Stewart, Tabori & Chang, 2007.

Gaughan, Norah. *Knitting Nature.* New York: Stewart, Tabori, & Chang, 2006.

Moreno, Jillian, and Amy R. Singer. *Big Girl Knits: 25 Big, Bold Projects Shaped for Real Women with Real Curves.* New York: Potter Craft, 2006.

__. *More Big Girl Knits: 25 Designs Full of Color and Texture for Curvy Women.* New York: Potter Craft, 2008.

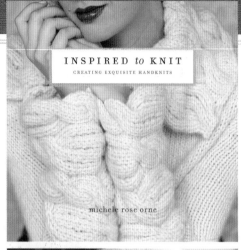
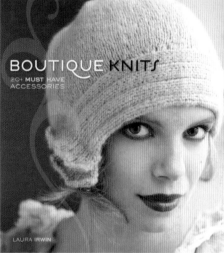